Discover
BestPossible Living

BestPossible Publishing

Discover BestPossible Living

Always a Way, Never too late

The BestPossible Series
Volume One

Eugene L. Bryan, PhD

BestPossible Publishing

Copyright © 2017 by Eugene L. Bryan, PhD
All rights reserved.

No part of this book may be reproduced or transmitted in any form or by any means, electronic or mechanical, including photocopying, recording, or by any information storage and retrieval system, without permission in writing from the publisher.

BestPossible® trademark is registered by Eugene L. Bryan.

ISBN-13: 9781976387364
ISBN-10: 1976387361

Library of Congress Control Number: 2017914269
CreateSpace Independent Publishing Platform
North Charleston, South Carolina
Printed in the United States of America
Order at www.amazon.com

Printed by CreateSpace, an Amazon.com Company
Charleston, South Carolina

*To Elaine Sivers Bryan,
my full-of-life, wonderful wife,
and to all who live in tune with Mother Nature*

Call to Action

All forms of life are naturally equipped for optimal living. Plants survive and thrive by biological programming. Animals do the same by instinct. Only we humans survive and live by freewill. We are on our own to **discover BestPossible living**. Read on to find your path of least resistance.

Contents

Acknowledgments ············· xv
Preface ··················· xvii
Introduction ················ xxiii

Part One — Wonders of Human Nature

Chapter 1 — The Power of Purpose ········ 3
  Nature-Based Life Purpose ············ 5
  Freewill Life Purposes ·············· 6
  Faith-Based Purposes ··············· 10
  Journeys through Time ·············· 11
  Self-Creation ··················· 12
  BestPossible Lives ················ 12

Chapter 2 — The Nature of BestPossible ······ 15
  Life's Continuum ················· 16
  Destination BestPossible ············· 16
  Fields of Opportunity ·············· 20
  BestPossible Is Forever ············· 21

Chapter 3 — Our Gift of Freewill ·········· 23
  Nature's Anomaly ················· 23
  Nature's Entitlement ··············· 26
  Becoming BestPossible ·············· 27

Chapter 4 — The Creation of Circumstances · · · · 31
- Blank Slates · 32
- Early-Life Programming · · · · · · · · · · · · · · · · 32
- Freewill Takeover · 33
- Creating Circumstances · · · · · · · · · · · · · · · 34

Chapter 5 — Gifts of Cognition, Thought, and Reason · 39
- Our Natural Tool Kit · · · · · · · · · · · · · · · · · · 40
- Awareness through Cognition · · · · · · · · · · · · 41
- Guidance through Thought and Reason · · · · · · · · · 42
- Liberation of Education · · · · · · · · · · · · · · · · 43
- Our Problem Solvers · · · · · · · · · · · · · · · · · 44

Chapter 6 — Rewards of Success · · · · · · · · · 45
- The Profit Imperative · · · · · · · · · · · · · · · · · 45
- Laws of Profit · 47
- Spiritual Wealth · 48
- Wealth of Resources · · · · · · · · · · · · · · · · · · 49
- Peace and Prosperity · · · · · · · · · · · · · · · · · 50

Part Two — The Nature of Self-Creation

Chapter 7 — Your Artistic Self · · · · · · · · · · · · 55
- Your Masterpiece · 56
- Benevolently Optimistic · · · · · · · · · · · · · · · 57
- Essential Roles of Role Models · · · · · · · · · · · 58
- Adding Depth and Color · · · · · · · · · · · · · · · 59
- Self-Esteem · 60
- Social Reflections · 60
- Creating Days and Years · · · · · · · · · · · · · · · 61

    Makeovers 62
    Tidying and Decluttering Your Masterpiece 64

Chapter 8 — Your Philosophical and Psychological Selves 67
    Five Questions 69
    The Nature of Philosophy 69
    Nature's Perspective 74
    Your Evolving Philosophy 75
    Your Psychology 75
    Psychology of Self-Esteem 77
    Psychology of Optimism 78
    Ambient Happiness 79
    Your Moral Compass 81

Chapter 9 — Your Spiritual and Physical Selves 83
    Your Spiritual Self 84
    Your Physical Self 86
    Naturally Free and Independent 87

Chapter 10 — Your Rational and Emotional Selves 89
    Joint Roles of Reason and Emotions 90
    Emotional/Physical Feedback 90
    Value Judgments 91
    Value-Based Emotions 91
    Rational Freewill 93

Chapter 11 — Your Social Self 95
    Gregarious Living 95
    Natural Morality 96

    Natural Relationships · 100
    Your Civic Self · 100
Chapter 12 — Your Enterprising Self · · · · · · · · · 105
    Entrepreneurial Start-Ups · · · · · · · · · · · · · · · · · · 105
    Modes of Life Management · · · · · · · · · · · · · · · · · 106
    About Constraints · 109
    Opportunity-Based Life Management · · · · · · · · · · 110
    Selective Service · 110
    Fiscal Independence, Spiritual Freedom · · · · · · · · 111

Part Three — Your BestPossible Self
Chapter 13 — The Magic of Now · · · · · · · · · · · · 115
    Revisiting Your Past · 116
    Inventing Your Future · 117
    Living in the Present · 123
    Mastering the Magic · 126
Chapter 14 — Purposes, Goals, and Waypoints · 129
    Finding and Serving Purpose · · · · · · · · · · · · · · · 129
    Creating BestPossible Beacons · · · · · · · · · · · · · · 133
    Waypoints and Mileposts · · · · · · · · · · · · · · · · · · 135
Chapter 15 — Your Life Journeys · · · · · · · · · · · · 137
    Joint Travels through Time · · · · · · · · · · · · · · · · · 138
    Artwork in Progress · 140
    Worldly Journeys · 141
    Inner Journeys · 145
    Balancing Your Life · 147
    Quality of Life · 148

Chapter 16 — Three Golden Keys · · · · · · · · · · · · · 149
   Golden Key One — Be Your BestPossible Self · · · · · 150
   Golden Key Two — Live BestPossible Days and
   Years · 152
   Golden Key Three — Celebrate Your Successes · · · · 155
   Your Golden Key Ring · 155

Chapter 17 — Taking Flight · · · · · · · · · · · · · · · · · 157
   The Four Forces of Flight · · · · · · · · · · · · · · · · · · · 158
   Licensed to Fly · 161
   Preflight Checklist · 163
   Flight Management · 165
   Smooth Landings · 166
   Soaring with Eagles · 168

Chapter 18 — Nature-Based Conclusions · · · · · · · 171
   BestPossible Living is Natural · · · · · · · · · · · · · · · · 171
   Your Masterpiece · 173
   BestPossible in a Troubled World · · · · · · · · · · · · · 173
   Master of Destinies · 174
   Continuous Liberation · 174
   On the Bright Side of Life · · · · · · · · · · · · · · · · · · · 175
   BestPossible Is Forever · 175
   Nature's Call to Action · 176
   In Harmony with Nature · 176

Epilogue — Dreams of the Future · · · · · · · · · · · · 177
Endnote · 181
Appendix A Chapter Highlights · · · · · · · · · · · · · · 183
   Part One – Wonders of Human Nature · · · · · · · · · 184

Part Two – Nature of Self-Creation	190
Part Three – Your BestPossible Self	196
Appendix – B Relevant Resources	**209**
Books	209
Documentary Films	210
Internet Websites	210
About the Author	**211**

Acknowledgments

First and foremost, I thank my ever-loving wife, Elaine, for her many supportive roles in my life and career. Her editing, proofing, critiques, and suggestions have been invaluable for writing all my BestPossible-based books—especially this one on discovering BestPossible living, to which she devoted much time.

Over five decades I have enjoyed working with hundreds of enthusiastic clients—firms ranging from family-owned companies to international corporations. I thank them for their innovative applications of my BestPossible concepts. Their progressive leadership, dedication, creativity, and field-tested suggestions have greatly contributed to the art and science of enterprise optimization.

Many have contributed valuable lessons and inspiration to what I now think of and spiritually enjoy as my wonder-filled BestPossible life journey. Among these are the wholesome post–World War II citizens of Paso Robles, California (a community of 5,500 when I moved there from Southtown Chicago at age eleven with my family). There I gained great lessons about nature and life from joining the Boy Scouts of America. It was also there where I learned the value of doing my one life right from Mr. Foster Jordan on his nearby wheat farm.

Finally, I wish to thank all authors of the books I've read that in some way promote wholesome, nature-based living.

Gene Bryan

Preface

*Look deep into nature, and then you
will understand everything better.*

—ALBERT EINSTEIN

Summer of '42

The roots of this book reach back to the early days of World War II. During San Francisco's summer of 1942, I was eight years old, the middle of five kids. We were a poor military family of the Great Depression, living in a housing project near the city's Cow Palace. Our unit was next to John McLaren Park. I enjoyed climbing trees in the park's wooded hills and was known to be the best tree climber of our neighborhood.

On the first Fourth of July after Pearl Harbor, a brass band drew me to nearby Visitacion Valley Park. The cool morning air bristled with patriotism. Soldiers, sailors, and marines proudly wore dress uniforms. Families were setting up picnics as their kids ran off to join in fun and games.

There were several cash-prize contests, but the greased pole was for me. There, the first kid to climb a ten-foot pole and claim the small American flag taped to its top would win three silver dollars—a small fortune in those days. A bunch of kids were lined up taking repeated turns. The problem was that whenever a climber gained a little traction, the man in charge regreased the pole as high as he could reach.

As I studied what looked impossible, I came up with a plan. First, I let kids go around me in line until I faced a freshly greased pole. I made an earnest first attempt before walking away covered with grease from head to toe. After rolling in the playground's sandbox, I timed my next try to be soon before the next greasing.

I can still see that little flag waving gently against a clear blue sky as I pulled it free. The clapping and cheering of the crowd made me feel like a changed person. I was. I still wore patched Salvation Army clothes, but inside I sparkled with what's-next excitement.

My "what's next" was to use my pole-climbing winnings to start my first business. I quickly enjoyed success as a shoe-shine boy. I could hardly wait to get going each day. I liked helping my family make ends meet, but mostly I loved the independence and responsibility that came with having and managing my own money.

One afternoon at the foot of Market Street in front of the Ferry Building, I shined shoes for two sharply dressed sailors. I asked one about the *E* patches he and his buddy wore. He told me they showed that their ship flew the "*E* for Excellent" flag. They and their shipmates had won a *Battle-E* competition for keeping their ship and crew ready for top performance. He said, "When going to war, we have to be the best we can be, and besides, it makes all of us feel good about ourselves, and that's half the battle."

Without knowing it at the time, my little business had just become a near-perfect win-win enterprise in which my greatest profits came in the form of indelible life lessons. Looking back I now see that my greased-pole climb and shoeshine business were kick starts for what has turned out to be a highly rewarding life.

Summer of '52

The summer of 1952 was another pivotal time in my life. After graduating from California's Paso Robles Union High School, I had the pleasure of working for Mr. Foster Jordan on his dryland wheat farm. At the end of a hard day's harvest, I asked, "Mr. Jordan, I've never seen you upset; how do you stay so cheerful, even when things go wrong?"

I will never forget his answer. "Gene, when I was a young boy, my father told me, 'We only get to live once.' After concerned thought, I decided that if I do it right, once could be enough."

That summer I had the privilege of working for a man skilled in what I now call BestPossible living. I left his farm determined to learn how to do my life right.

Although it was not until 1986 that I coined the term *BestPossible* and started using it in my work as a pioneer in the field of computer-based enterprise optimization, it is a label that fits nature's plan for all life forms. Early in my fifty-year career in this field, I realized that the enterprise we can call *life management* involves more issues and complexities than those faced by the largest corporations. At the same time, I realized that most of my enterprise optimization and BestPossible concepts can be applied to help a person make his or her life the best it can be. It was then that going for BestPossible was what Foster Jordan called "doing life right."

Lessons since my entrepreneurial youth surely led to my choice of careers. In my early years, I thought this was merely about high achievement; I now know working toward BestPossible achievements means learning to recognize and follow nature's path of least resistance to optimal success. It's about working to identify and capture the best of opportunities along our life journeys.

I share these boyhood stories and career experiences to give you a peek at the genesis of this book and my ever-rewarding discovery of what I like to call the magic of Destination BestPossible.

Shades of Gray

The start of this book dates back thirty-five years. I was using the working title *Shades of Gray* to write about how my enterprise-optimization concepts can be used to help people find their way through the fog of the complexities of life management. While attending a writer's conference in San Diego in the summer 1982, I was introduced to Ken Blanchard[†] and his literary agent, Margaret McBride. Encouraging meetings and discussions with Ken, and later with Margaret, led to what turned out to be a thirty-five-year journey of study, research, concept development and refinement, and finally writing and publishing the book in your hand, *Discover BestPossible Living: Always a Way, Never Too Late*.

[†] Author of *The One Minute Manager* with coauthor Spencer Johnson.

Deep into Nature

Dr. Albert Einstein profoundly observed, "Look deeply into nature, then you will understand things better." It seems I was looking into nature throughout my boyhood and looking even more deeply during my dual careers as a scientist and an entrepreneur. With this book I am pleased to share some of the most important lessons and knowledge I have gained from my fascination with and focus on nature.

You are likely to find that most what of you read and discover seems to be common sense. If so, that is because most comes from my observations of nature. I have worked to stay away from conjectures, suppositions, and subjective opinions. Consequently, I am hopeful you'll find much to absorb without argument: being immersed in nature and her universal laws is as close to truth and reality as we can get.

—Gene Bryan

Introduction

Dost thou love life? Then do not squander time, for that is the stuff life is made of.

—Benjamin Franklin

If there was a sure way to make the rest of our years the best they could be, who would not choose to go that way? Good news! There is such a way, and it is actually nature's intended path for all humanity. Because we are born with only one life to live, BestPossible living makes good sense, and it's not as hard as it may seem. Living in harmony with nature and going with the flow of nature mean enjoying paths of least resistance.

I coined the word BestPossible (BP) to name a superlative beacon for all occasions, all endeavors, and all our journeys through time—long or short. I first intended the word to be a noun, but it was soon used by my clients as an adjective (as I have used it in the title of this book) to label plans, teams, and resources put together to achieve BestPossible, the noun. It was a long time before I realized my new word puts a handy label on what has been nature's intent for all life forms from the beginning of time.

What I call BestPossible is best visualized as a beacon that guides our way along a purposeful journey through time. Think of all our purposeful endeavors as subjourneys, each with its own self-envisioned and self-defined Destination BestPossible.

One of best things about BestPossible is that the closer we get, the better it gets; with every step forward, we gain experience, wisdom, perspective, and resources to push what's possible toward ever-brighter horizons.

BestPossible living is living with purpose and defining our goals in order to be the best we can achieve. Between where we are and where we could be are unique fields of opportunity ripe for harvest. As we progress and make our BestPossibles better, we uncover fresh opportunities for even greater fulfillment, joy, and happiness.

We move and live in the direction of our focus. Without positive goals, pessimists live with expectations of darkness. So-called realists reside within their comfort zones as they miss opportunities to add rewarding depth and color to their lives. All the while optimists expect and enjoy bright-side living. The focus and goals of optimists move them naturally toward waypoints along paths leading to their BestPossibles.

Just as success is a journey and not a destination, BestPossible is not about arrival; it's a way of life. This means the joys of BestPossible living begin the day you decide to go for the brightest horizons you can imagine being reachable.

Introduction

BestPossible is time dependent. You can go for BestPossible days, weeks, months, years, and the rest of your life. You can get started by deliberately making each of your tomorrows as good as you can envision it to be.

Wouldn't it be great if our schools taught young people how to stay in harmony with nature as they shape the lives they choose to live: how to create and enjoy BestPossible lives? The six chapters in part 1, "The Wonders of Human Nature," explore some of the lessons we could have been using to great advantage had we not missed this kind of life primer during our school days.

Everyone's life consists of a series of parallel and divergent journeys through time. In part 2, "Nature of Self-Creation," you'll find six chapters that cover key aspects of ourselves that we are free to develop to help make all our journeys as successful and rewarding as they can be.

Our lifetimes have three dimensions, and truly BestPossible living requires good use of all three. The magic of now allows us to gain more from our pasts, live our presents more fully, and invent our futures to be what we choose them to be. In the six chapters of part 3, "Your BestPossible Self," I describe how you can use 3-D time travel to great advantage when going for your various BestPossibles.

Each of us inhabits two worlds: an inner world under our control and an outer world that is subject to our influence. Our outer worlds are filled with noise, clutter, and distractions that take time and energy away from the health and wellbeing of our inner worlds. Deliberate BestPossible living allows us to enjoy the best of both worlds as we change and to enjoy our private inner worlds while doing whatever we can to make our outer worlds better places to live.

As you will discover, BestPossible can serve well as a mantra for a new way of life. Covering key aspects of day-to-day living, this book offers insights and proven systems you can put to immediate use for BestPossible life management.

Some readers will be readier than others to embrace and use this book's insights. But because all its messages are founded on natural laws and the basics of human nature, *Discover BestPossible Living* offers value to people of all ages, genders, races, colors, religions, national origins, and levels of education. All humans already reap rewards with every step they take toward the bright side of life. Here you'll learn how to make your steps more deliberate and your rewards more plentiful.

Every aspect of our lives—such as family, health, wealth, and career—has its own shades-of-gray continuum with BestPossible at its bright end. When we learn how to recognize and capture opportunities in one area, there is natural carry-over into others. For this reason going for BestPossible in one dimension becomes a training ground for living on the bright side in all we choose to do.

The potentials for personal achievement are virtually limitless. So why don't we achieve more? It is because we hold ourselves back by self-imposed restrictions, irrelevant comparisons, and excuses. Satisfied we are doing quite well and better than most, we stop far short of BestPossible.

Introduction

To be the best we can be, we need to think and act far beyond our current perceptions of what is possible and certainly beyond the expectations of others. This may sound like a lot of work, but BestPossible achievements are more fun and less draining than struggling to keep up. World-class athletes, artists, and other performers enter harmonious zones where everything seems to flow effortlessly. As we become skilled in the art of BestPossible life management, we, too, can break free of conflicts, frictions, and wasted energy. Deliberate journeys to BestPossible can put us into special zones for smooth, efficient, and highly rewarding performance.

Mother Nature means for our lives on Earth to be wonderful and exciting, and it's up to each of us to make them so—for ourselves and others. Wonder dissipates, and excitement fades when we stand still. We need change for inspiration. Doing business as usual is a mode of false security for watching opportunities and life pass by. To keep wonder and excitement alive, we must move toward brightness in all that we do.

This book is not just intended to help you be more successful in specific pursuits. As you work deliberately to make your life shine, look around, and be proud. You will witness transformations that help brighten paths for others around you; journeys to Destination BestPossible yield widespread rewards.

Whether nature comes from a supreme creator, from evolution, or from a combination of causes, it is what it is: it's to be seen, studied, recognized, and honored—or not.

This fact that nature exists independent of personal beliefs and perceptions means the insights and lessons of this book can be studied, accepted, and applied by readers of all persuasions, religious or not.

Readers who like to study tables of contents for previews may choose to start by reading this book's appendix of highlights for helpful terminology and subject orientation and for an unusually thorough preview.

One of the most inspiring books of all time is James Allen's 1903 classic *As a Man Thinketh*. After Allen's 1912 death, his wife, Lily, wrote, "He never wrote theories, or for the sake of writing; but he wrote when he had a message, and it became a message only when he had lived it out in his own life, and knew that it was good. Thus he wrote facts, which he had proven by practice." † In this same spirit, for the same reasons, and by the same means, I offer *Discover BestPossible Living* as a book based on proven, easily observed truths of nature.

† James Allen, *As a Man Thinketh* (2017).

Part One

Wonders of Human Nature

Quite surprisingly and wonderfully, Mother Nature has been equipping humans with tools and incentives for BestPossible survival and advancement for more than fifty thousand years.

BestPossible is a universally applicable concept for all human endeavors. Our freewill † lets us think, make decisions, and act during our time in this world as prosperously and enjoyably as possible. The more skilled we become at leading optimal lives, the more we are able to contribute to the wellbeing of our communities and nations and the entire world.

† Although not the most common spelling, *freewill* as a one-word noun works more cleanly and effectively for the context of this book.

Chapter 1

The Power of Purpose

*Our lives are strings of purposeful actions.
We determine the quality of our lives
by our choices of purposes and their
resulting actions and achievements.*

Action powers changes—some minute, some major, some profound in their lasting effects. Our travels through life are composed of purposeful actions that determine our net levels of inner peace, prosperity, and quality of life. This means our purposes are the primary factors in determining how well we live our years.

Recognized or not, every human action has purpose. From the rhythmic beats of our hearts to our pursuit of lifelong missions, we act involuntarily or deliberately with purpose.

Our physical selves connect our inner selves to the material world in order to pursue purposes. The more clearly we understand what we are doing and why, the more deliberately we pursue our objectives and the more certain and rewarding our outcomes. This applies to all pursuits, from putting on our shoes in the morning to working to achieve our most ambitious lifetime goals. For BestPossible living defining purpose and goal setting will rank at the top of all skill sets.

Our choices of purpose are literally infinite. So how do we decide what to do with our days and lives? This question and its answers are of utmost importance: they determine what kind of people we become and how we live our lives. This is why and where our freewill gains its greatest significance. Nature gives us freewill to give meaning to the concept of freedom and to give us control of our lives. BestPossible living requires self-control in the sense that we must consciously choose our own purposes and act accordingly. With every moment of every day, we advance in time. If we are to advance in a direction we want to go, we must be careful and deliberate in our choices of purposes.

So once again, how do we decide what to do with our days and lives? The answer isn't really how *we* choose; each of us must answer individually. A dominant purpose of this book is to help my readers explore options and choose BestPossible purposes for their daily, yearly, and lifetime endeavors.

The most important issue is how wholesome our purposes are. To live good lives, we must be good people with wholesome values and motives. This requirement sounds easy, but

Part One—Wonders of Human Nature

because of our freewill choices, we face temptations that can lead us far astray.

Nature-Based Life Purpose

According to nature's plan for our time on earth is to practice BestPossible living. This serves nature's purpose of peaceful and prosperous propagation of her most complex of all life forms.

By genetics or instincts, all plants and animals are naturally equipped for BestPossible success. Plants use best-available sunlight, water, soil nutrients, and atmospheric carbon for BestPossible production of a cornucopia of fruits, fiber, refreshed air, and seeds for endless propagation. Birds live BestPossible lives from the energy they put into their feeding, nest building, and migrations. For survival and growth, animals optimally gain more energy than they expend in their foraging and hunting.

We humans, too, are equipped for BestPossible living, but as anomalies of nature, we survive and advance toward BestPossible only through freewill and choice. In our use of our nature-endowed mental tool kits and our freewill, we must remain ever vigilant to avoid natural temptations that draw us toward darkness. Nature allows us to fail or achieve high levels of success; she leaves it up to us to master our tool kits to live close to BestPossible lives.

Nature's plan is our reality; the forces and laws of nature can be ignored but only at our peril. Eventually, Mother

Nature will have her way. This fact is the basis for all chapters of this book. When we live in tune with nature's plan, we advance toward brightness; when we work counter to her laws or try to change them, we inevitably drift toward darkness. It's our choice in all that we do.

Given the above a nature-based life purpose can serve as a generic foundation for all people who choose to live as wholesome contributors to their communities, their world, and their own wellbeing. Near the end of their days, this foundation will allow its subscribers to say:

* I am pleased with how I've lived my life.
* I have been a good, honest, wholesome person who has been generous with the joy and happiness I've shared with others.
* I have few regrets.
* I have made a difference for many worthy people.
* I have loved being alive and free to pursue and share the happiness I have enjoyed along my life's journey.

Freewill Life Purposes

By way of our freewill, we are responsible for choosing the purposes that determine all our actions and the quality of our lives. Beyond a wholesome foundation, we get to add unique flavors that come with our freewill pursuits.

As we define our values and purposes and chart our courses, we must first learn the differences between right and wrong, between good and evil, and between love and hate. Through observations of causes and effects, we can learn a lot about nature's plan for BestPossible living.

Right versus Wrong

There is an easy way to tell right from wrong based on the nature that surrounds us. It is based on the miracle of life. Right versus wrong is a moral issue tied to life. In the absence of life, there is no moral issue. What promotes life is right; what detracts from life is wrong. For example, if I were to crush rocks, my act would be neither right nor wrong; rocks are not alive. But if I were breaking rocks to make gravel to keep my family from slipping on deadly ice, the issue of right versus wrong clearly comes into play; now crushing rocks becomes a good action, as it could help preserve life.

When we face the complexities of life, things can get confusing because we are surrounded by shades of gray. In high school I enjoyed a required class called Senior Problems. One day we were asked to describe the difference between love and infatuation. When I offered my carefully considered answer, our teacher said, "Gene Bryan, you seem to see everything in black and white; our world isn't like that."

I replied, "When we run into shades of gray, shouldn't we try to sort the black from the white?" I don't remember her exact answer, but it was something about that not being possible. I didn't, and still don't, believe that. The more important the issue, the more essential it is that we do such sorting and act accordingly. We can't always avoid gray, but it's important to be aware and weigh the effects of compromises.

Wrong   **Right**

Decision Continuum

Whenever we face a decision, we have a purpose. If we can't avoid compromise, the right choice is the one that best serves our purpose, all things considered. That will be a BestPossible answer because it considers unchangeable circumstances.

Good versus Evil

When discussing and naming good and evil, there are no shades of gray. A person's purposes and actions either promote lives in tune with nature or they work against her. Good people sometimes do bad things by mistake; evil people repeatedly do bad things on purpose; they use their freewill to work against nature.

Evil   **Good**

Human nature is such that evil people pursuing faulty results enjoy emotional rewards when their despicable acts succeed. This is where—being anomalies of nature—people can feel happy while advancing toward their own rewards and the demise of others'. To avoid this trap of nature, we must avoid embracing wrong values—those that are not wholesome promoters of life.

Fortunately, evil people are vastly outnumbered by good people who have nature on their side. While the destruction and death caused by evil may slow the positive march of civilization, eventually nature will have her way as she rewards goodness and works to squelch evil motives.

In the context of this book, there is no place for wrong and evil motives and actions. When going for BestPossible, any movement toward darkness would be a blatant contradiction of intentions.

Love versus Hate

Both love and hate are emotions that come from value judgments. This is their only similarity. Love is the ultimate in benevolence; hate is the ultimate in malevolence. Love is the most life promoting of all emotions. It is experienced as a positive, healthy emotion that is right and good in every way. Love resides at the bright end of life's emotion continuum.

Hate is love's direct opposite. It is the darkest of all emotions. Contrary to promoting life, hate works against it in every way. To harbor hate is to deliberately wreak havoc on one's emotional wellbeing, along with all the detrimental hormonal implications. Hate is a choice that makes no sense. To consciously choose to be an unhappy, hateful person defies all logic. Why do it when there's so much about life to love? What's even worse is to hate unknown people and situations based on the value judgments of strangers and pundits with agendas that are not your own.

Like evil, hate resides on the dark side of life, as far as one can get from BestPossible living.

Faith-Based Purposes

About 84 percent of the people in the world follow one of 4,200+ religions. It is likely that, with a few exceptions, the beliefs and teachings espoused by these religions are consistent with the nature-based life purposes described above. This is because their faith in God or some other supreme being means an acceptance of nature along with her laws and ways.

Further, faith-based purposes do not invalidate or deny time for freewill-based purposes. We have to act while in the here and now as we serve our primary life purposes. If your freewill choices are aligned with what you determine to be the will of God, you'll be richly rewarded for your successful steps along your earthly journeys.

Part One - Wonders of Human Nature

Journeys through Time

Movement in status is a journey through time. People perform best when they can visualize where they have been, where they are, and where they are going. This journey concept provides a natural metaphor for life management. Instant failure or success seldom happens; we slide defensively toward failure or advance proactively toward higher levels of success. The vision of journeys allows people to see what's going on, turn around when moving in the wrong direction, and redouble their efforts to get further ahead.

All our life's endeavors can be viewed as journeys through time, represented by shaded continuum with BestPossible on the bright end. Chapter 15 shows continuum for common journeys that we travel over our lifetimes. You can follow these examples to create your own family of continuum for estimating starting positions and logging the progress of your set of key endeavors.

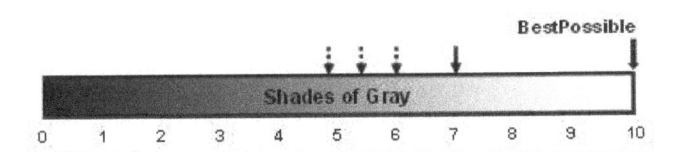

```
                                              BestPossible
                          ↓ ↓ ↓    ↓              ↓
        ┌─────────────────────────────────────────┐
        │           Shades of Gray                │
        └─────────────────────────────────────────┘
        0   1   2   3   4   5   6   7   8   9   10
```

Our subjourneys, too, are travels through time. Most of us will face challenges, ever-unfolding opportunities, thrilling adventures, and disappointing setbacks for actions based on our freewill choices. If we choose wisely, our actions will be subservient to our lifelong purposes; they will serve as the means to achieving what we want in our lives.

Self-Creation

The power of purpose is felt up close and personal as we shape who we are and how we choose to live. From how we look after our health and fitness to our choices of careers and how we otherwise invest our time, we are involved in a continual process of self-creation. I have selected and organized the contents of this book to serve as guides to help readers deliberately choose their purposes and thus create in themselves the people they would like to be. This is not a difficult task. It actually calls for living in harmony with nature and following paths of least resistance.

BestPossible Lives

What is a BestPossible life? Each of us will answer with what counts most to us. For me this kind of life is where and when a person's inner self is free of unhealthy worries and stress: a life based on a wealth of wholesome relationships and personal freedom, productivity, and independence. Such spiritual selves know and enjoy high levels of day-to-day happiness that come with well-earned self-esteem.

As with most things in nature, the normal distribution of our nation's adult population's quality of life, as measured by one's inner peace and ambient level of happiness, will follow a common bell-shaped curve in which 2.5 percent will enjoy lives to the right of two standard deviations. With our nation's 2017 adult population estimated at 260 million, this would mean a little more than 6.5 million people are already living what we can reasonably call BestPossible lives. This large number is not surprising given nature's intent.

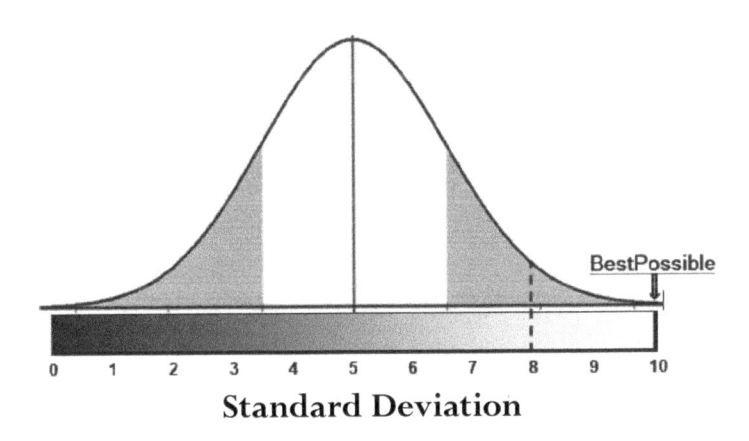

Standard Deviation

This graph is included to show you that you won't be a lone soul in going for BestPossible and that it's not an impossible dream. Those who achieve an 8.0 or higher on the quality-of-life scale are surely among those who are enjoying the rewards of living in tune with nature.

Quality of Life

Discover BestPossible Living

Discovering and creating purpose are the primary keys to optimizing your life. You can make it happen by tapping into high-voltage power of purpose. By choosing your most dominant purposes to be aligned with your envisioned BestPossibles, you will surely find yourself enjoying the rewards of BestPossible living.

Chapter 2

The Nature of BestPossible

*BestPossible is not something to do until
something better comes along. In the here
and now, nothing can be better.
But our BestPossibles get better as we get better.*

We only get one life to live. We hear people rightly say, "This is the first day of the rest of my life." In the context of this book, this is an observation that applies to us all. It says, "From this day on, things can and will be different." This is true—by design or default—but your days will be much better by design. We can choose to make the rest of our life journeys as good as we can make them. To do so, we need to first recognize the remaining part of our life journey will be composed of thousands of subjourneys as we take on countless life-sustaining and life-enhancing endeavors. This is good news in that it means we will be living and enjoying life one manageable bite at a time.

Life's Continuum

As we traverse along on our journeys through time, it helps to visualize our advancements as movements away from darkness toward brightness—along shades-of-gray continuum where every step is in a healthy, life-enhancing direction.

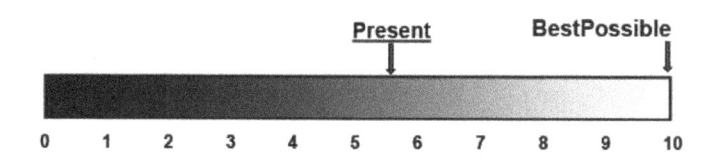

For every endeavor from the most trivial to the most profound, the continuum metaphor works well to envision progress, slippages, and current positions relative to BestPossible. To focus attention on our most important dimensions of life, I suggest you use this continuum-based visualization concept as a position-tracking process at least for your basic journeys as covered in chapter 15.

Destination BestPossible

For our successes to be meaningful we must have destinations; actions without purpose are wastes of time. Beacons are like lighthouses that lead us in safe travel as we enjoy successful steps along our way. When we purposefully craft our

Part One—Wonders of Human Nature

goals to be the best we can conceive as achievable, we can more confidently and assuredly move toward what we want our destinies to be.

Although lighthouses still have nostalgic value, they have been largely replaced by GPS navigation. Once we specify a destination, this highly precise satellite-based technology instantly locates our present position and shows us how to most quickly and safely get to where we want to go. But it is still up to us to name our destination and to start and continue the journey.

Because BestPossible living is nature's intent, most people naturally set out to do the best they can when undertaking an important task. The differences between implied and deliberate efforts partially explain why relatively few folks lead BestPossible lives while others fall somewhere nearer to average along the bell curve of population distribution. Explicit goals serve better than random travel.

For my 1942 Fourth-of-July pole climb I was deliberately striving to achieve what I now call BestPossible. My goal was to retrieve that little American flag to exchange it for the prize of three silver dollars. (As it turned out, I went home with the money and the flag.)

My next major achievement was earning my Eagle Scout badge. During the last two years of World War II, my father served on Chicago's Navy Pier, and our family lived in the city's nearby Southtown. At the war's end, we moved to Paso Robles, California, where I made friends with a neighbor Boy Scout named Jay. Although I was not quite the then-required age of twelve, Jay took me to a Scout meeting and loaned me his *Boy Scout Handbook*. I learned about the ranks and requirements of Tenderfoot, Second Class, First Class, Star, Life, and Eagle Scout. Considering the time required to go through the ranks and earn twenty-one merit badges, I figured I could make Eagle before my fifteenth birthday. I set that as my BestPossible three-year goal. With pursuit of every rank and merit badge as a mini journey, I enjoyed what surely could be called BestPossible living.

Whoever first said that "success is a journey, not a destination" understood a lot about life. But even though our rewards come along the way, we need destinations to give our journeys purpose and meaning. Based on my pole climb, my scouting days, my academic achievements, and my business successes, I can vouch without hesitation the truth of the following attributes of Destination BestPossible:

1. **Universal**—Destination BestPossible is a beacon for all human endeavors and organizational missions. But these missions are universal in concept only. We all have a unique BestPossible for each of our endeavors, such as earning a merit badge, picking a church, choosing a career, planning a vacation, or creating the kind of person we want to be.
2. **Honorable**—Destination BestPossible applies only to worthy, honorable endeavors and missions. It makes no sense for bad or evil objectives.

Part One—Wonders of Human Nature

3. **Self-Defined**—Every person has a unique, optimal level of performance defined by his or her purpose, capabilities, and circumstances. Only you know your purposes, aspirations, priorities, levels of ambitions, and current circumstances.

4. **Time Dependent**—Every BestPossible's time frame ties to its purpose. It can extend a day, a week, a month, a year, or a lifetime. We can also have achievable waypoints of variable time frames to serve as interim BestPossibles along main journeys through time. This means we can enjoy success from day one and all along our way.

5. **Inspirational**—BestPossible is a highly motivating and inspiring goal. Just as Mother Nature provides rewards for success as incentives for more success, so does working toward becoming the best we can be. The same applies to working to become better because becoming better requires steps toward brightest possible horizons.

6. **Rewarding**—All steps forward deliver inevitable rewards of success. When you set a BP as your goal, your material and psychological rewards become amplified as you approach your destination.

7. **Always a Way, Never Too Late**—BestPossible is an always-attainable goal; that's the special meaning of the two-word noun. It is, by definition, achievable no matter the person's present position. It marks what is possible, all things considered—including all current circumstances such as opportunities, capabilities, and

limitations. Also, by definition, it is never too late to go for BestPossible.

Fields of Opportunity

Between our present position and BestPossible are all our opportunities for improvement; there is no place else to look. Within these fields are many kinds of opportunity. These include simple versus complex, easy versus hard, strategic versus tactical, big versus small, and ripe for harvest versus can wait.

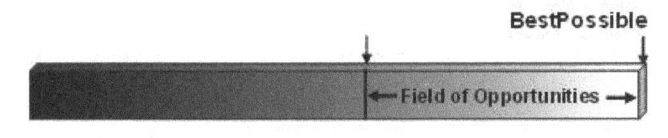

BestPossible
← Field of Opportunities →

Achievement Continuum

Wherever you are on your continuum at the moment, please recognize that between where you judge yourself to be and your self-defined BestPossible is your ready-for-harvest field of opportunity. This field is not debatable; it is within the scope of what you have envisioned to be possible. Some of your opportunities will be much greater than others, and some will be easier to capture.

Pareto's principle is commonly translated into an 80/20 rule. Applied here it would suggest that 80 percent of our fields of opportunity can be traversed using 20 percent of the effort it would take for full harvest. If this is true, then careful setting of priorities can speed your progress toward BestPossible.

BestPossible Is Forever

BestPossible is forever in two ways. First, BP is not something to do until something better comes along. By its definition nothing can be better. Fads come and go, but basic truths stand unaltered by time; there is and always will be a BestPossible level of achievement for every undertaking.

Second, BP is forever because, as we approach it, a new and better BP appears on the horizon. As long as we are advancing on worthy missions, we will enjoy growing reserves of ideas, wisdom, and resources that allow us to advance without end.

Chapter 3

Our Gift of Freewill

We humans are nature's only creatures who survive and advance by freewill. This means we have to choose to live BestPossible lives. It also means there is no limit to how great we can make our lives.

We all have requirements for survival and advancement and endowed mental tool kits of natural abilities; how well we learn to use our tools determines our levels of success. Whatever our current purpose and endeavor, our decisions and actions determine where we reside on our achievement continuum.

Nature's Anomaly

An anomaly is defined as a deviation or departure from a normal order; it's an irregular, abnormal occurrence. Among all living creatures, we humans are anomalies of nature. It's as if we came from a different planet. This has its advantages and disadvantages, but it is what it is, so we'd best learn the pros and cons of this reality and get on with making the most of living prosperous, happy lives.

There are many ways we differ from all other life forms. The freewill requirement of human survival and advancement is our basic anomaly, and it leads to all others. Awareness of all irregularities can serve us well by providing advantages for the many dimensions of our lives and for erecting safeguards against ever-present natural traps. With such awareness there is much we can and should do to optimize our time on planet Earth. Here are some ways our freewill makes us anomalies of nature:

1. Self-Creation

Rather than acting by instinct or according to biological programming, we must act by choice, and our choices are, by design or default, value based. This makes us vulnerable to bad value judgments and poor or destructive choices.

On the positive side, this anomaly allows us to discover and embrace a unique set of values to guide our choices throughout our lifetimes. It is this anomaly that allows us to make ourselves into the people we want be and to choose and enjoy very happy lives.

2. Morality

Only we humans face the question of morality. Of all life forms, no others must choose between right and wrong, good and evil, and love and hate. In creating ourselves, our value judgments and moral choices predetermine the levels of success and happiness we will know in our lives.

But there is good news in our freewill: we can always correct mistakes, change course, and get on track for BestPossible living. For us humans predetermined is never permanent. As the saying goes, "There's always a way; it's never too late."

In chapter 8 you'll learn about the nature of morality and how we can safeguard our actions to avoid falling into life-limiting and destructive traps.

3. Natural Traps

Only we, of all life forms, can act toward our own destruction while enjoying the process right up to our demise. Again, because of our freewill, we can make faulty, destructive value judgments. And because achieving and embracing values brings us happiness, flawed reasoning and the resulting positive emotions can work together to lead us into harm's way.

Secondhand living is the most common and harmful of natural traps. It occurs when people embrace and live by values that do not come from firsthand value judgments but instead are based on the desire for popularity and acceptance. "Keeping up with the Joneses" is a common example. But secondhand living afflicts people unsure of themselves in thousands of ways.

Rationalization makes an unreasonable position or act appear reasonable. It is often used to let seemingly honorable ends justify dishonorable means. Unfortunately, the best rationalizers are smart, creative people who can easily recruit less astute secondhand-living victims to join flawed causes.

All-too-common natural traps are indoctrinations by way of propaganda and outright brainwashing. Here again uninformed secondhand living makes people vulnerable to being used to accomplish the unsavory agendas of others.

4. Masters of Destiny

Perhaps the most positive aspect of being anomalies is that we are, by design or default, masters of our own destinies. This applies not only to our overall life journeys but also to our parallel and side journeys. As long as we can exercise our freewill, we are responsible for our choices and actions, as well as their outcomes.

This fact is especially relevant in the context of optimizing our lives to become our BestPossible selves. As the masters of our various destinies, we are free to choose to become whatever kind of people we would like to be.

Nature's Entitlement

Along with endowing us with basic tools for survival and advancement, Mother Nature grants us only one entitlement: freewill. She expects us to use our brains and bodies to sink or swim, with her intention being that we swim exceedingly well.

Part One-Wonders of Human Nature

There is good reason we are born with freewill as our only entitlement. It's the only way we can grow into responsible adults, independent of others for our survival and advancement. As we meet and handle life's challenges, we gain the experiences, knowledge, wisdom, and self-esteem to blossom and prosper. This frees us all to experience the joy and rewards of life without being burdens to others.

Nature's single entitlement translates simply into freedom, liberty, and opportunity. When we let our governments create welfare programs and other entitlements in the name of compassion, we endorse robbing Peter to pay Paul. This goes against nature in that it takes fruits of the labors of some while depriving others of their primary sources of self-worth and enjoyment.

Compassion comes one person at a time from individual value judgments. We are compassionate beings by our human nature; we naturally want to help good people who have temporary or permanent needs they can't satisfy by themselves. Wholesome human beings value the lives of others; they help not out of entitlement but out of their love of life.

Becoming BestPossible

We are constantly *becoming*; nobody stays the same from day to day. Our decisions and actions inevitably change our inner and outer states of being. To choose to become BestPossible is a long-term and, hopefully, lifelong commitment. You'll never arrive because with your advancements will come gains that make your BestPossibles better. But that's OK; you will always be enjoying the successes and rewards of your various life journeys.

As you gain experience and skills along the way, you'll discover two ever-present hallmarks of BestPossible living:

1. **In Tune with Nature**—Because it is nature's intent that we all live BestPossible lives, you'll find that following her lead will take you along the paths of least resistance. You'll discover it is best not to resist or fight her—morally, ethically, physically, or spiritually.
2. **Optimistic**—A dominant hallmark of BestPossible living is enthusiastic, reality-based optimism. The reality comes from the fact that all goals are self set to be achievable. Optimistic enthusiasm is continually fed by the endless rewards of achievement.

Along the shades-of-gray continuum, pessimism, so-called realism, and optimism reside from left to right. Expectations affect outcomes. I was once a diver on a swim team. I quickly learned that when launching off a springboard, the body goes where the head goes. The same happens in life. People who look toward the dark side of life tend to get a lot of what they expect. Those who see their comfort zones as reality tend to stay close to their reality with passive acceptance.

Optimists proactively exercise their freewill and continually choose to become happier, more fulfilled participants in

Part One—Wonders of Human Nature

life. That's what becoming BestPossible is all about: It's not about arrival. It's about living and enjoying the journey.

Although we humans are innately equipped with all the tools we need to live at the BestPossible ends of our many continuums, we come into the world without instructions. Each of us must learn how to use our tool kits, even as we face a world of endless possibilities and hazards. How well we do this determines our levels of success and happiness along our life journeys.

We can achieve BestPossible in things we choose to do. But because we live by choice and freewill, we must first learn what is possible and then how to make it happen.

Although plants and animals have the advantage of being preprogrammed for optimal success, we have something much better. Whereas their standard of success is survival, our standards reach out to focus on quality of life and happiness. For this we are blessed with freewill and opportunities to reach far beyond mere survival to make our BestPossibles whatever we choose.

Chapter 4

The Creation of Circumstances

BestPossible recognizes all circumstances. The better we plan and control our circumstances, the better our BestPossibles.

Our earliest beginnings are of course beyond our control. But once we discover our nature-endowed free-will, we start shaping our own lives. Even then we can be victims and benefactors of circumstances. But most often our circumstances can be traced to our own decisions and actions. This is a reality that is essential to recognize in the context of becoming our BestPossible selves.

Except for acts of nature, what we attribute to happenstance can be traced to actions and decisions of people. While we think of seemingly random occurrences as the result of unavoidable accidents or some kind of good or bad luck, they seldom are. More often they result from the cumulative effects of past decisions, actions, and defaults of ancestors, parents, civic leaders, and others who have shaped our cultural environments. The nature of happenstance is not so much random as the result of the obscure causes and effects of prior choices and actions—our own and those of others within our spheres of activity and influence. This is important to keep in mind as you consider the many ways circumstances affect our levels of success as we work to gain more direct control of our lives.

Blank Slates

The circumstances of our birth, of course, greatly affect our start in life and perhaps eventually the levels of our BestPossibles. Our DNA and other genetic factors depend on the family histories of our mothers and fathers.

Our gender, race, country of birth, and family economic status all come together to determine and influence what kinds of challenges and opportunities we face at the time of our birth. Aristotle's tabula rasa (blank slate) concept is likely true, but the circumstances of our birth certainly affect how we begin working on our blank slates.

Early-Life Programming

From the first days of your life, preprogramming began. How you were held and loved by your mother and treated by your father, siblings, and others started a preconditioning of your sense of life. As you grew through childhood into adolescence, for better or worse, you were subjected to the values, religions, and politics of your parents, other family members, and close friends.

Depending on the pace of independent thinking, you started to question your preprogramming as you began to become your own person. If you were fortunate enough to avoid most of nature's traps, you were on our way to using your freewill for creating your own purposes, plans, happenings, and circumstances.

Whatever your beginnings please know and remember this: your freewill allows us to break free and become whoever you choose to become. This will be harder and more challenging for some than others, but by awareness and determination, it can be done.

Freewill Takeover

As a sophomore in high school, I began to seriously question my own preprogramming and wanted to know more clearly how I should be living my life. I had serious questions about my church's teachings, my school lessons, my relationships, and many other issues. One day to deal with these concerns, I mentally stripped the Earth of everything manmade and then slowly added back only things that made sense to me. I called this my zero-based value project. I was surprised and comforted by how much popped back into play. Food, clothing, shelter, and transportation were obvious examples, but so were most institutions including schools, churches, and governments. I found good reasons for arts, sports, and recreation. Happily, I found the shared love and joy of close relationships essential for giving life purpose and meaning.

This was a good, sobering exercise. It gave me a close-up look at nature and all that we humans have that adds excitement and quality to our lives. Dr. Einstein said, "Look deep into nature, and then you will understand everything better." My zero-based value exercise did in fact help me understand what really counts at an important point in my life. I learned a lot about the nature of reality.

While not many are so deliberate in questioning what has been handed to them, all of us go through a process of creating our own person, along with a set of values to serve as our moral compasses. Without such a deliberate questioning process, we would be forever vulnerable to being used and abused to serve the wills, motives, and agendas of others. The nature-based lessons of this book are offered to help you escape flawed preprogramming to achieve more rewarding freewill takeover in planning and managing your life.

Creating Circumstances

James Allen's classic book of essays *As a Man Thinketh* is delightful in how well it shows that our thoughts create our predominant circumstances. First we think and dream (visualize); then we plan and act. Our plans and actions put into

Part One—Wonders of Human Nature

motion the forces that set the stage for favorable circumstances. For example, say you need money to start a business. Your business plan attracts potential investors and opens doors for eventual win-win circumstances.

When we hear of happenstances, we often think of good or bad things occurring beyond our control. This is sometimes the case, but more commonly our circumstances are of our own making. When we plan ahead, we set things in motion that determine what we do, who we meet, and where and how we play our game. All our plans and actions tie to our self-chosen and crafted paradigm, and it is here we set wheels turning to set up our most determinate circumstances. With purposeful planning and action, happenstances can become part of the scenery we can enjoy or handle along the way to our destination.

Passions and Purposes

I once had the privilege of hearing one of the most successful businessmen in Oregon speak. When he opened the meeting for questions, the first came from a man in the front row who asked, "I came today hoping to learn your secret for success. I've heard a lot of good ideas, but can you briefly summarize your secret?"

Without hesitation the man answered, "Find your passion, and live it!"

Because this speaker was a close friend, I knew his advice was about more than business success. This man was one of the most generous, compassionate people I I had ever known. He had earned substantial wealth, but more importantly, he enjoyed inner peace, fulfillment, and happiness.

The circumstances of our lives uncover and grow our passions and lead to our choices of purpose. This applies especially in our early years, but it holds true as long as we hold lust for life. This fact is highly important when working to discover the best ways to direct our activities and invest our time. Ultimately, our levels of achievement will be measured by the health of our inner selves—by the degrees of fulfillment and happiness we feel and enjoy. The greater our passions and the clearer our purposes, the greater our spiritual rewards.

By choosing and creating circumstances according to our interests and talents, we are likely to find fertile ground for passions to grow while we identify and pursue enjoyable missions. This is very much a key to controlling our destinies, and it starts with creating BestPossible sets of circumstances. This calls for harvesting from within best-available fields of opportunity.

Planned and Unplanned

It's usually better to face planned, rather than unplanned, circumstances, but either can prove to be advantageous. Planning is all about predetermining circumstances. When things go as planned, everything falls neatly into place. When things go wrong, it's often due to unexpected occurrences. Sometimes this brings unfolding opportunities.

Opportunities and Limitations

Unplanned circumstances present us with new opportunities and limitations—and often some of both. Unfolding opportunities are most often unexpected; they happen regularly and offer individuals and organizations near-term ways to improve. For example, when I was nine months short of completing the requirements for my Eagle badge, my troop's scoutmaster resigned and moved away. As senior patrol leader for our troop, I convinced Mr. Campion, our council's scout commissioner and our Methodist church sponsor, to allow us to continue meeting. To make sure our conditional approval was not revoked, I called on my troop to shine. For what turned out to be almost a year, our troop 36 won the highest honors at every regional camporee. The loss of our scoutmaster turned out to be a blessing. It gave our four patrol leaders and all their scouts a goal and the determination to make our team the best it could be.

When working toward a BestPossible goal, we must be watchful for new, unplanned ways to make our goals and potential achievements ever better.

Unexpected limitations most often are temporary constraints on progress that can be creatively overcome or circumvented. Through this process, limitations can very often be transformed into opportunities.

Adjusting and Changing Course

No matter how good our initial planning, changes happen that call for adjustments or complete changes of course.

In my professor days, I served as adviser for several dozen students. Many were unsure of their desired fields of study. These were individuals who were more influenced by parental expectations than their still-to-be-discovered interests and passions. I shared my fictional "A Short Tale of Two Cities" with each of these young adults. My story is about a recent graduate of Humboldt State University who had learned of a great opportunity in New York City. He mapped a course from Arcata, California, that took him over Donner Pass to Reno, to Salt Lake City, and through Denver. While enjoying a cup of coffee, he read in the *Denver Post* of a better opportunity in Miami. Changing his goal and course didn't diminish the excitement and reassuring feedback he enjoyed traveling and reaching his first three waypoints.

Until you discover something more exciting, staying on the course that's BestPossible at the time is the right thing to do. What's not good is to keep on keeping on when your interests, passions, and heart are calling you elsewhere. Course adjustments and changes are normal parts of optimal living; it's a process of gaining advantages from the unfolding of unplanned, unforeseeable circumstances and opportunities.

Chapter 5

Gifts of Cognition, Thought, and Reason

Our nature-endowed tool kits serve many functions. Two master tools coordinate all others. These gifts are to be nurtured and cherished all the years of our lives.

The 2013 movie *First Footprints: The Original Pioneers of All Humankind* is a wonderful documentary that shows how, starting fifty thousand years ago, we humans have been successfully pioneering for survival and advancement. From these ancient beginnings to now and forever, all human actions and accomplishments can be attributed to a combination of three drivers: purpose, cognition, and reason. Without purpose, nothing desired can be made to happen. Without cognition and reason, there would be no deliberate positive change.

We simultaneously live in our private inner spiritual world and our shared outer material world. To facilitate her plan for BestPossible living and in recognition of the freewill of us humans, Mother Nature has equipped us with the tools we need to connect our two worlds so that we can observe, perceive, reason, decide, and act in ways that lead first to survival and then to the security of advancement and BestPossible living.

We are naturally equipped to enjoy a high quality of life, but our tool kits come without instruction manuals; it is up to each of us to learn their use and find our way. Besides having parents, teachers, and others to help us, we have nature-based emotions as feedback for trial-and-success lessons.

Nature has an unwritten, unforgiving book of rules we must discover and follow if we are to live and flow in tune with her plan. Again, we are well equipped to discover and follow her rules, but we must do so by freewill.

Our Natural Tool Kit

Our brains are unbelievable in what they do—and in what they can do that we too often leave neglected. While they remain busy taking care of our bodily functions, they stand ready to serve our developmental and social needs. To maintain control of our wellbeing, we need to proactively use our minds to direct our freewill. But too often we default to judgments and choices of others as we go about creating who we will be and choosing the courses we follow.

Part One–Wonders of Human Nature

For BestPossible living we need to become skilled in using our natural tools:

* Senses of sight, touch, hearing, taste, and smell
* Perception
* Cognition
* Memory
* Thought
* Reason
* Emotion
* Creativity

These tools are life essentials, but all can be misused. For example, we can misperceive or misinterpret the evidence of our senses and make serious errors of thought and action. As another example, we become vulnerable when we make decisions based on emotions instead of reason.

We have these tools from birth, but it is up to each of us to learn and, in time, master their use. This is especially true for cognition and reason because we use these abilities to integrate our other tools to gain knowledge and wisdom and to solve problems we encounter throughout our lives.

Awareness through Cognition

Of the above list of tools that come with our nature-endowed tool kit, cognition and reason are heavy hitters. Cognition is a natural and often an involuntary (intuitive) process of acquiring knowledge of our outside world. Consciously and subconsciously, we use cognition to integrate prior knowledge, memory, and sensory inputs to help us make decisions, solve problems, and guide our lives. We use our cognition to become and stay aware of our surroundings and their relevance to our lives. This natural gift allows us to acquire knowledge, understanding, and wisdom through a mix of focusing, thinking, remembering, reasoning, making decisions, problem solving, and other things we do in the process of managing our lives.

Significantly, in this book's context, cognition is an educational tool: with it we can use what we already know to know more. Cognition utilizes all pieces of our tool kits to enable us to direct our freewill for BestPossible living.

Guidance through Thought and Reason

Through the processes of thinking and reasoning, we consciously make sense of important aspects of our inner and outer worlds. Using logic and facts, reasoning allows us to look after our own interests as we serve the needs and wants of others. The use of reason combined with cause-and-effect observations allows us to discover what is right and wrong, good and evil, and true and false. Clearly, thought and reason are among our most important mental tools. Our thoughts direct our focus and trigger our reasoning. These are tools we should use regularly and consciously for guidance as we navigate through life's challenges and pitfalls. Enlightened

Part One-Wonders of Human Nature

reasoning is what we need in order to capture the best of our fields of opportunity along our journeys to BestPossible. Thought and reason are essential keys for freedom, liberation, and self-determination.

Liberation of Education

Our education starts at birth and grows throughout our lives. Whatever our goals, improved cognition, reasoning, and gained knowledge broaden our fields of opportunity. The more deliberate, focused, and skilled we become at acquiring knowledge, the greater our sources of fulfillment and happiness.

During my time as a university professor, I advised my students to learn a lot about the world around them with priorities based on proximity. Our daily actions are directed at serving the needs and wants of ourselves and others. We serve best when we have a good understanding of the people and communities in our lives. Education links us to all that we do.

Much of what we learn comes to us from our outside world as we attend the school of life. Here our lessons come unfiltered. This is where we must use our cognitive skills and common sense to help determine the worthiness and relevance of our chosen relationships, purposes, and missions.

Among the many good things that come from the school of life is language. Without it we could not function socially or intellectually. Words are like little suitcases that store and carry concepts for use when we need them to form thoughts and to communicate. Without words we can observe, but we cannot think and converse. The more extensive our vocabularies, the deeper our thoughts, the greater our creativity, and the better our contributions to our communities will be.

Literacy is important for communication and especially for learning. Being able to read opens a world of information we can use to enhance our lives. As we grow our vocabularies, we more broadly open our world.

Our tools of cognition and reason serve us best when we learn how nature works and how we invariably suffer when we act against her.

Our Problem Solvers

How well we learn to live and enjoy our years depends greatly on how well we learn to use our nature-endowed tools, especially our gifts of cognition and reason. These are and always will be our primary problem solvers; they connect our inner and outer worlds and enable us to perceive, decide, and act in our own best interests as we optimally serve the needs and interests of others.

Chapter 6

Rewards of Success

With every success comes a spiritual and material profit. We need profits of both forms to fuel our life journeys.

All life forms require profit for survival and advancement. This means that profit motives are essential parts of human nature. Without profits there would be no life on Earth. Nature promotes all forms of life with its flawless incentive plan that inspires action by rewarding success. In short, profit is the fountainhead of life—no profit, no life. Fortunately, nature offers an abundance of opportunities to profit and prosper from noble, life-sustaining pursuits.

The Profit Imperative

Without fail, nature rewards the successes of honorable endeavors. Of all subjects, perhaps the most important to place and keep in good perspective is the crucial role profit plays in our individual lives. Without profit, except for natural formations, all that we enjoy would not exist—including life itself. Profit is nature's way of assuring continuation and advancement of life. Profit, in its many forms, inspires action by rewarding success. As nature's profit plan works to assure survival of the fittest, it provides incentive for improved fitness. The extent humankind has advanced beyond its primitive origins reflects how well we have learned to work with and enjoy the rewards of nature's laws of profit.

Plants profit from their use of sunlight to transform water, soil nutrients, and carbon dioxide (CO_2) into a cornucopia of fruits, fiber, refreshed air, and seeds for endless propagation. Birds profit from nest building and the energy they put into their migrations. For survival and growth, animals must gain more energy than they expend in their foraging and hunting. Life of all forms depends on the endless pursuit of profits. Security, freedom, and joy that all extend beyond mere survival come in direct measure with the successes of those pursuits.

For us nature offers endless challenges and commensurate rewards as incentives for action. When successful we profit physically, emotionally, and materially from our investments of time, effort, and resources in our many life-promoting pursuits. Failure is nature's way of signaling faulty motives and methods so that we can make adjustments and reverse course. The laws of the universe are always in play to reward our successes and to provide lessons when we get off track.

Part One—Wonders of Human Nature

Laws of Profit

Universal law is part of nature and is binding upon human actions. The law of gravity cannot be escaped; besides holding the universe together, gravity's ever-present forces make all known forms of life possible. This basic law, like all others, rewards adherence and punishes denial.

Many of nature's laws have been explicitly recognized and named. Others have not, but they demand adherence all the same. I was surprised when my Internet search for "law of profit" came up empty.. I suspect life's dependence on profit is so obvious that it has escaped formal recognition. Based on observation and simple logic, I have identified, defined, and named three corollary natural laws of profit as follows:

> **The first law of profit**: Survival requires that the sum of gains be at least equal to the sum of expenditures during life-sustaining activities.
>
> **The second law of profit**: Security requires a sum of gains greater than the sum of the expenditures required for survival.
>
> **The third law of profit**: Advancements come in proportion to net gains beyond requirements for survival.

Material wealth includes assets available for development or investment and is a sign of the financial strength of individuals, organizations, and nations. This straightforward definition is fitting for the context of this book. Such material wealth stands as the primary means for advancement of civilizations. The human corollary to material wealth is the spiritual wealth of individuals. Material and spiritual wealth depend on and inspire each other. And together they confirm the third law of profit.

Spiritual Wealth

Our inner worlds need care. The workings of our brains are marvelously mysterious in how well they perform their many life-sustaining functions. Even though they are material in form, their functions are very much spiritual: we can't find or see our memories, thoughts, passions, or aspirations.

The three laws of profit apply to both our material and spiritual worlds. While material gains are important, and often essential, for advancement, only our spiritual rewards shape what really counts when all is said and done. Other than making us happy and adding the self-esteem that comes with personal achievement, fancy cars and big houses are nothing more than stuff. It's how they make us feel that matters.

Spiritual profits of success include the following, among many other things:

* Inspiring feelings of self-worth
* Happiness
* Inner peace
* Motivating for further success
* Added knowledge and wisdom

Nature is always at work steering us toward BestPossible lives. With our failures come rewards in the form of incentives to make corrections and act more in tune with the realities of nature. Our negative incentives include these:

* Diminished feelings of self-worth
* Sadness
* Inner disappointment
* Added knowledge and wisdom about what doesn't work

Our spiritual rewards and lessons work to promote Mother Nature's plan. By rewarding success and steering us away from failure, she is doing her part to promote good action, to discourage and minimize mistakes that good people make, and to punish the bad behavior of evildoers.

Wealth of Resources

Some material rewards of success are enjoyed right away, but many are amplified as resources that we use to create more success. A resource is anything we have or can acquire to serve a purpose. Resources enable our missions. The better we become at acquiring and using resources, the closer we will come to achieving BestPossible performance in all that we do.

We can divide our resources into six basic classifications:

1. **Knowledge:** education, experience, skills, common sense, wisdom
2. **Capital:** money, credit, land, material wealth

3. **Associations:** communities, churches, clubs, teams
4. **Opportunities to provide service:** associations, jobs/careers, family, friends, self
5. **Creativity:** Natural and developed talents to use resources to innovatively achieve specific purposes
6. **Options to acquire resources:** Available but untapped sources of all the above

As we work to optimize our journeys, we need to regularly look beyond resources on hand to include those we can acquire. This applies to all six classes. We advance by the strength of our resources and our knowledge and skills in using them. To advance substantially we must add to our strengths, knowledge, and skills.

These six classes of resources are universal and basic. Among these classifications are all the things we have available to achieve our missions.

It is important to keep in mind that all classes of resources work together to affect our outcomes. But it is also good to know that it is this network of resource relationships that generates the complexities of life planning and management.

Peace and Prosperity

With a continuing stream of profits come peace and prosperity. This is true for all life forms but especially for us humans. When we gain from our efforts, our worries and stresses

Part One-Wonders of Human Nature

diminish as they give way to positive expectations and encouragement for more efforts.

Profits are near-term physical and mental rewards that provide incentives to stay actively alive and involved. Prosperity is a state of flourishing that comes with ongoing successes and their flow of profits and acquired resources. All come as peaceful spiritual rewards and worldly external rewards. Please note that peace feeds prosperity, and prosperity feeds peace; they always work together and are always tied closely to our profit imperative.

Part Two

The Nature of Self-Creation

*Through her gift of freewill, Mother
Nature has enabled each of us to create
the person we choose to be.*

The lessons of the six chapters of part 2 are a compilation that offers big-picture insights on what you can do to optimize your life journey and subjourneys throughout your time on earth. Mother Nature intends for you to live BestPossibly and has equipped you with all that's necessary to do so. In the section that follows I briefly cover six primary aspects of your life with nature-based guidance for creating and continually becoming the BestPossible you.

Chapter 7

Your Artistic Self

We are all artists, and our most important creations are ourselves. Each of us is a work of art that will be a work in progress throughout the years of our lives.

Everyone is born with consciousness and creativity. From birth all people naturally observe, perceive, imagine, and imitate role models as they learn to love, walk, talk, and start a lifelong process of creating the person they choose to be. We all start life with the same set of mental tools; how well we master our gifts of cognition, thought, and reason determines the character of our most important work of art and the quality of our lives.

Everything we think, do, and say throughout our lives affects what kind of person we will be at any point in time, in some measure. But our memories fade and are altered based on new, wiser perspectives. There are things we've done in the past that we would never repeat and things we

Discover BestPossible Living

failed to do that we would not miss a renewed opportunity to rectify. This means that even as we carry our fading pasts, our creations of ourselves as works of art are—and forever will be—works in progress. This means we can always do BestPossible makeovers.

Your Masterpiece

Your masterpiece starts with your thoughts. Whatever you're thinking, doing, or saying, it is good to keep in mind that you are an artist at work creating who you are and will be. This is a heavy responsibility that few people realize. The more deliberate and conscious you are about your thoughts and their resulting choices and actions, the more your masterpiece will be by design rather than default. You'll become more of a firsthand person rather than a secondhand reflection of other people's values.

You shape and color your character through your family interactions, friendships, education, work choices, and all forms of social involvement.

Recognized or not, we all use role models to help us choose what values to embrace. The more conscious we are of the role models we choose to emulate, and why, the more we will retain control of our wellbeing and destiny. Importantly, we have to be careful that our choices fit our purposes and passions.

Your artwork and resulting character will first and foremost reflect your basic values. These in turn will show in your deeds, integrity, and wholesomeness and in the health of your worldview. Most importantly, your basic values will determine your levels of success, happiness, and fulfillment throughout your days and years.

When you do a great job on your masterpiece, you will be a source of enjoyment for those close to you, like all good artwork. This will become increasingly so as you add color and depth to your character through your humor, friendships, job experiences, travel adventures, sports, readings, recreation, and myriad other activities.

Benevolently Optimistic

Important parts of your character show physically in your demeanor, laughter, posture, and manner of speaking and in many other subtle ways. But what makes up your true self are your core values; they illuminate your sense of life and how you view the world.

If your core values are in harmony with nature, you will have a benevolent and optimistic attitude toward life and all it has to offer. You'll focus first on what is good about the world around you with confidence and realistic expectations of success. People with malevolent and pessimistic views of life are likely to be afflicted with negative emotions and are vulnerable to unhealthy feelings and behavior. Nature is all about survival and advancement—conditions that are consistent with benevolence, optimism, love, compassion, and high expectations.

Essential Roles of Role Models

You shape and color your character through your family interactions, friendships, education, work choices, and all forms of social involvement. Recognized or not, we all use role models to help us choose what values to embrace. The more conscious we are of which role models we choose to emulate, and why, the more we will retain control of our wellbeing and destiny.

When we were born, we started life with a blank slate of values. Rather than having to reinvent the wheel, we had people around to serve as role models to accelerate our preparation for independent living. Even as infants we started exercising choices of role models as we favored those who generously gave love and happily received ours. As young children our cognition kicked in as we quite naturally learned how to discern between good and bad, between right and wrong.

As children we grew more adventurous and subject to temptation. Lacking experience and wisdom, the complexities and risks of adopting and choosing values led us into a wilderness of exploration and experimentation. This happens for better or worse, and it adds great importance to art of self creation.

Creating your own person is first about thinking, reasoning, choosing, adopting, and embedding core values and then adding excitement, color, and texture by your choices of personal values.

No one creates their person from scratch; nor should they. Life has too many options and too little time to live by trial and error. Role models can appear in the form of other

Part Two-The Nature of Self-Creation

people or as their lessons and accomplishments as found in books and lectures. Your masterpiece will be totally authentic—free of plagiarism and forgery—as long as you learn from wholesome, happy, wise people who live or have lived according to life-promoting core values.

There's no reason to limit the number of your role models. Among my own are Leonardo da Vinci, Michelangelo, Adam Smith, Benjamin Franklin, Thomas Edison, Albert Einstein, Milton Friedman, and of course Foster Jordan.

Adding Depth and Color

We add depth and interest to our characters through diversity of experience. By way of our friendships, education, reading, travel, and vacations, we create in ourselves new dimensions to our beings. As we add to our repertoire of experience, we open doors for gaining knowledge and wisdom that continually broaden our fields of opportunity and add to the ways we make our BestPossibles better.

Here I speak from experience. I've lived in thirteen states and more than thirty towns and cities—a result of being from a military family followed by independent moves as an adult. While working my way through four university degrees, I've enjoyed the privilege of having held many jobs. With each move and every new job, I added depth to Gene Bryan as I enjoyed my life more fully.

A happy person is a colorful person. Why is that? Happy people radiate energy that brightens rooms and the people around them. If you ask kids with boxes of crayons to draw a happy person, they naturally choose bright, exciting colors—no others would work. Children understand happiness.

Your life is yours to color as you please. The more colorful you choose to be, the more success you'll enjoy.

Self-Esteem

Your self-esteem is hidden within your inner self, but it's an essential aspect of your masterpiece. Although invisible to the world, it openly reflects your overall evaluation of your own worth and attitude toward yourself. When we value ourselves, we act to advance our lives. We gain self-esteem as we demonstrate to ourselves we are able to successfully act to acquire and protect what we value.

Self-image and self-esteem play integral roles in your life. By building your self-esteem, you enhance your expectations of your future. You add to your self-esteem by staying true to your moral compass and choosing and achieving worthy and noble purposes.

Social Reflections

We can't see our values when we look in a mirror. We see only our physical selves and not our inner spiritual selves. When we meet people for the first time, though, although we do see them physically, we see much more. Their inner masterpieces are visible through their levels of presence, expressions, postures, mannerisms, eye movements, strength of voice, and other subtle projections. We use our cognition to pick up on what's important and what these signals means to us—namely, how they match or conflict with our values. Through mutual projections and reflections of shared values, we form alliances and find friendships.

Because we are all artists, we naturally show our values in our work. When others respond favorably to our creations, it is because they share at least some of our core values. Benevolent people of wholesome values naturally attract other good people.

Creating Days and Years

Our artistic selves have our outer worlds to tend to. Knowingly or not we all create, every day and year of our lives. Being at the helms of our lives, we are the ones who must steer our way into the future. We can leave the task unattended or abdicate the helm to others but not without negative consequences. We may rightly choose to follow others' suggestions, advice, and invitations but only with conscious awareness and good reason.

To live BestPossible lives, we must create and plan each of our days, weeks, months, and years according to self-chosen purposes from among our personal fields of opportunity. Like many people, my wife creates all her days by way of to-do lists. She takes pleasure in crossing through items as she gets them done. If there are things she's not able to get to, she moves them to the next day. She uses her electronic calendar for weekly, monthly, and yearly planning.

Makeovers

Depending on your starting place, your artwork may be a makeover more than a from-scratch composition. Either way the rewards for success can be just as satisfying.

Perhaps the most remarkable makeover in the realm of art is Michelangelo's creation of David. At the age of twenty-five, he contracted to take on a long-neglected, partially started, giant piece of weathered marble called The Giant. He transformed it into a seventeen-foot-tall statue of the biblical hero David. For two years he chiseled away every bit of marble that didn't fit his image of what he wanted.

The message here is that as you take on personal makeovers, you will very likely have to chisel away a lot of previously embraced values and relationships that don't fit the image of the kind of person you want to be.

We come into this world as blank slates that are analogous to the blocks of marble a sculptor uses to create

Part Two-The Nature of Self-Creation

artwork. But we must work well beyond three dimensions. (In chapter 15 you'll find continuum covering fourteen universal dimensions.) Our media is more malleable and our mistakes more correctable. Our self-creations are of utmost importance in that they determine the courses and successes of our lives. As we work to reshape who we are, which we can do at any time along our way, we must be watchful to avoid taking on false values. It is easy to make false starts and more difficult to escape them.

Successful makeovers are hard but very gratifying; with clear vision and conviction, makeovers are possible. The process happens all around us every day. That's what exercising our freewill is about.

BestPossible living comes as result of creating and being a BestPossible person. This has nothing to do with perfection. Instead, being a BestPossible person means being and enjoying the doable person you prefer to be.

Remember, success is a journey, not a destination. You can enjoy every part of your masterpiece even as you are making it over. There are rewards for doing the best you can to be enjoyed every day.

The good news is that we are forever works in progress. We change every day as we have new thoughts, make decisions, and gain experience from the things we do. This means we are not strangers to the makeover process. What's important is that we have plans and conviction—that we do our makeovers by design, not by default.

Tidying and Decluttering Your Masterpiece

Marie Kondo's 2014 best-selling book *The Life-Changing Magic of Tidying Up* has been published in more than 30 countries with sales exceeding four million copies. Clearly her lessons deliver much value to her readers. While her book is mostly about how to tidy and declutter your home, Ms. Kondo in effect shows how laws of cause-and-effect come into play to magically bring peace, joy, and prosperity to one's mind.

What is the *cause* and what is the *effect*? Does a cluttered mind cause a cluttered home and workplace or vice versa? The answer is both. It's hard to keep thought purposeful and organized when surrounded by clutter and a disturbed mind's priorities are likely to neglect picking up and keeping things organized. Either way there is good reason to keep your character and abode free of mess and distraction.

Messes and distractions come from undisciplined thought, lack of purpose, worry and fear, pessimism, and all other manners of negatives. Such causes sneak into our minds, lives, and characters unnoticed and insidiously set up roadblocks to BestPossible living. As creators of ourselves and as works-in-progress we must remain ever-diligent to avoid unhealthy thoughts, choices and actions.

The main point of this chapter is that your life is yours to create and shape as you choose: you are the artist in charge. If you choose to create and prepare yourself for BestPossible

Part Two-The Nature of Self-Creation

living, you can do just that. Please remember: there's always a way, and it's never too late.

The remaining chapters of part 2 cover five other key aspects of your person. As you read please keep in mind that they all ultimately become dimensions of your masterpiece. These key aspects all call for decisions that will directly affect your levels of success and the quality of your life.

Chapter 8

Your Philosophical and Psychological Selves

*Each of us has a philosophy. Without
one we would be adrift with no rudder or
anchor. We each have a psychology to help
us find our way and stay on course.*

Most of us are almost strangers to our philosophical and psychological selves; we don't know them well or what to expect of them. Going forward greater awareness of and better acquaintance with these two foundational parts of ourselves will help us maintain control and protect us from being manipulated to fit others' agendas.

You may find the fact that each of us holds a mostly unrecognized, yet critically important, philosophy and psychology a bit worrisome. But before you get too concerned, it is likely that yours have been and will continue to serve you quite well. That you are reading this book means you are probably reasonably aligned and headed toward bright horizons. Wherever you are in your life, the insight of this chapter will help you examine and hone your philosophy and psychology for more rewarding travel along your various journeys through time.

We head into life with philosophies and psychologies that are bits and pieces inherited from our families, friends, teachers, and community culture. Because we are immersed in reality from birth, much of our early-life programming is about survival, getting along, and getting ahead. By osmosis-like cognitive absorption, we learn a lot about what's right and good, what works and what doesn't, and how to be happily successful in much of what we do.

As we start exercising our gift of freewill, many of our initial choices and actions will be reflections of values we have picked up from others. As we gain experience, confidence, cognitive skills, and wisdom, we increasingly become our own persons.

No matter where we start out, we can reshape our philosophies, psychologies, and resulting value judgments at any time. There's always a way; it's never too late to realign. For example, I dramatically changed my worldview in the spring of 1946 when I left the World War II ghettos of Southtown Chicago to restart my life in the wooded hills and open spaces of small-town Paso Robles, California. I became a brand-new person ready to shape my future to be the best I could imagine.

Part Two-The Nature of Self-Creation

Five Questions

Recognized or not, your philosophy allows you to live within our universe and world without mind-messing distractions. Accurately or not, it provides answers to questions that free you to go about daily living:

1. What is real?
2. How do I know what is real?
3. What should I do about what I know?
4. How should I fit in and act among other people?
5. What kind of person should I choose to be?

The Nature of Philosophy

If Mother Nature were an actual woman, she would live by a philosophy that is totally aligned with that of Mother Nature, the nonperson. This is a circular way of saying that we can have a worldview and a way of life that are in constant harmony with the natural world around us.

There are five branches of the study of philosophy that pertain to the five questions I've listed above. All are parts of your philosophical self. Although they reside quietly in your mind, you'll soon recognize how important each is and how it affects the course of your life.

1. **Metaphysics**—This is the branch of philosophy that is concerned with existence and the nature of things that exist. Basically, it is a theory of reality that reaches out to

include studies of relationships between our minds and matter. Metaphysics looks to distinguish between what's real and what's not.

Ever since its naming about 2,300 years ago, the lasting question of metaphysics has pertained to whether reality is objective or subjective: Is it objectively real, or is it subject to the perceptions of its perceivers? For many, if not most, people, this is a silly question; of course reality is real! But many scholars and politicians prefer a subjective reality in which there are no absolutes, no right and wrong answers, where they can reshape and interpret nature in the name of justice and equality.

In his famous allegory, the ancient Greek philosopher Plato describes prisoners chained in a cave and unable to turn their heads. All they can see is the wall of the cave. Behind them a fire casts shadows of frightening figures on the wall they face. He used this scenario to show that reality is subject to how it is perceived. When I first read this so-called proof many years ago, I concluded that people can be deceived by magic tricks. The fire was real, and the images were made by real photons of light; what was not real was Plato's contrived context. Today we are entertained by magicians skilled in the arts of deception, distraction, and delusion. It is one thing to be entertained and quite another to become victims of con artists and others with costly ulterior motives.

Part Two-The Nature of Self-Creation

Here is another common example people use to question the objectivity of reality. They ask, "When a tree falls in a forest with no people to hear it, does its fall make a sound?" The reality is that the tree's fall disturbs the air with vibrating sound waves that move nearby objects, including hearing organs of all animal life, including bugs and birds. The fact that no humans are around does not alter the nature of reality.

2. **Epistemology**—This branch pertains to the theory of knowledge, especially with regard to its methods and validity. Epistemology is the investigation of what separates actual truth from unfounded opinion. It's about how we acquire knowledge through our senses; the forming and use of concepts; and the use of memories, logic, emotions, and other mental tools. It's about how our minds connect with realty in valid and life-promoting ways.

To survive and advance, we have an inherent need to know what to do. Not only that but to act decisively and confidently, we need to be sure of what we know. This makes the role of epistemology a critical branch of philosophy.

Reason and logic, science, empirical experience and observation, trial-and-error experiments, and common-sense cognition are all ways of gaining knowledge—some more reliable than others.

Many of us rely heavily on experience and common sense in learning how to stay in touch with reality. For example, we learn and know not to touch a hot stove and not to fall into the Grand Canyon. By trial and error, we learn and remember if we prefer chocolate over strawberry ice cream. By empirical evidence, we learn that air travel is faster and less fatiguing than driving. For more complex questions of reality, we have come to depend on science. But in all cases, we must rely on reason and logic for making safe, sound decisions. Emotion-based choices can be OK when triggered by memories of past successes, but they make us vulnerable to serious mistakes.

For some, epistemological faith is a contradiction in terms because of lack of evidence. However, faith has proved to be a highly valuable source of guidance throughout human existence. Faith allows people to live and thrive in the face of critical unknowns and unknowables. For example, ancient Egyptians attributed the flooding of the Nile River to the god Hapi. Unaware of upstream rainstorms, their faith allowed them to explain the dangerous floods as they received and farmed their annual heavenly gift of newly deposited fertile soil. Today about 84 percent of our world's population follows one of roughly 4,200 religions as they seek purpose, promise, and peace of mind.

The importance of epistemology in our view of reality is that we have a way of knowing truth from fiction as we exercise our freewill through the course of our lives.

3. **Ethics**—This branch of philosophy looks at the moral principles that govern a person's behavior when relating

Part Two-The Nature of Self-Creation

to others and conducting activities. It looks to define a system of moral values that are aligned with the nature of reality.

The concepts of right and wrong and good and evil are of course key ethical issues, but there are many others that affect our levels of wellbeing and our quality of life. Our moral values help determine our purposes, how we treat others, and our ultimate destinies. The more we understand about ethics and are able to deliberately keep ours exceptionally wholesome, the more rewarding will be our days and years.

4. **Aesthetics**—This is the branch of philosophy that pertains to the nature, perception, and creation of beauty. It studies psychological responses to artistic experiences.

All forms of art involve projections of human values. Because we can't see or touch a person's values to appreciate and endorse his or her existence, aesthetics plays the life-promoting role of letting us emotionally feel, experience, and celebrate the values of artists.

Creativity is art. Inasmuch as our freewill requires us to be creative, we are all artists, and we project our values with everything we do. (See chapter 7: "Your Artistic Self.") This makes aesthetics an essential part of our lives.

5. **Politics**—This branch of philosophy is about governments, liberty, justice, and the enforcement of codes of law. It is about ethics as applied to societies of people.

Politics speaks to the importance of getting metaphysics right. Anything less than full acceptance of the objectiveness of reality would allow desires and efforts to change nature into whatever one would wish it to be. Such thinking and attempts are, at best, formulas for failure, and too often, they lead to death and massive destruction.

Without valid perceptions of reality, politics will inevitably violate laws of human nature and abuse the concept of social ethics. Close examination of history's wars and resulting calamities shows that in all cases, tyrants acted against the laws of human nature. As an extreme example, the more than sixty million who were killed during World War II lost their lives because of the irrational motives of dictators acting against nature.

Nature's Perspective

For a simple explanation of the roles of philosophy, metaphysics asks what is real, epistemology asks how we know, and the other three listed branches ask what we should do about what we know.

In nature reality is what it is, independent of how it might be perceived by an individual or a majority of a society. As for the other four branches, nature's laws apply as they relate to the concepts of right and wrong and good and evil. (See Chapter 1.) Nature is foursquare behind a philosophy that promotes life throughout all its dimensions. If you want to embrace a BestPossible philosophy, try your best to learn and follow nature's lessons.

Part Two—The Nature of Self-Creation

Your Evolving Philosophy

How you see and relate to the universe is your philosophy. By far the most important part of your philosophy is metaphysics. It is the cornerstone of philosophy. How well you recognize and accept reality determines where you'll stand relative to nature on all other aspects of your philosophical alignment during the course of your life. The more clearly you see reality and the more purposefully you stay in tune with nature, the more rewarding your life journey will be. Just as BestPossible is forever, with ever-brightening horizons, so too can your philosophy be. It will evolve as you gain wisdom and make better value judgments.

I cannot overstress that there is always a way to achieve BestPossible and that it is never too late. Grandma Moses started her world-famous paintings at age seventy-eight. There are countless examples of criminals, addicts, abusers, and otherwise misguided people who turned around their lives to become productive, happy contributors to their communities.

Your philosophy will evolve throughout your life with your freewill choices and actions. The more you know and remember about this fact, the more you will stay in control of your circumstances, happiness, and destiny.

Your Psychology

Our psychologies are our mental characteristics and attitudes. All human behavior is psychological and subjective;

Discover BestPossible Living

one's actions are subject to one's personal perceptions of reality, purposes, experiences, priorities, circumstances, and a myriad of other factors.

How our objective outer world and our subjective inner world come together is the realm of the science of psychology. It is important that we perceive the outside world as the objective reality that it is—what we choose to do about it will and should be subjective, that is, subject to your purposes and values.

But we must avoid the trap of thinking all of reality is subjective. It is not! We can't make it into what we would like or hope it to be with impunity. Mother Nature will have her way; we can't sway her with wishes and denials. And that is as we should want it. We can do much better building our foundations on firm, solid ground than on delusional quicksand.

As covered in chapter 3, there are in fact reality-based consequential differences between right and wrong, good and evil, love and hate, truth and lies. If we are to live wholesome BestPossible lives, we must learn to perceive and accept reality as objectively reliable. Only then can we safely use our senses and psychological tool kits to subjectively tend to our purposes and priorities.

When it comes to BestPossible living, two of the most important aspects of your psychology are your levels of self-esteem and optimism. Ranking high in these personality traits is in fact prerequisite to enjoying a high quality of life.

Part Two-The Nature of Self-Creation

Psychology of Self-Esteem

Everyone has a hierarchy of values. Imagine what yours looks like: Near the bottom might be what you might buy at your local Dollar Store. Moving up would be the value you put on an hour of your time. High in your list of values would be major physical possessions, followed by friendships, and then loved ones. You could rationally sell your car or house to pay for an operation needed to save the life of your spouse but not to save a murderer; an exchange of a value for a lesser value would not only make no sense but would disarm the essential roles value judgments play in guiding our lives and actions.

At the top of everyone's hierarchy is one's self—its owner. When making value judgements, one cannot value anything more than oneself. The saying that we first love ourselves before we can love others comes directly from the psychology of self-esteem.

As a general rule this is how life works. There are, of course, complex exceptions where we may risk our lives for others or to preserve our freedom. My wife and I had the privilege of spending two hours with a World War II hero and Medal of Honor recipient. Mr. Robert D. Maxwell was in eastern France when he threw himself on an enemy hand grenade to save soldiers around him. Facing what appeared to be certain death, he, without hesitation, was giving his life for the value he had for his friends and country. He survived his wounds to live an honorable life of distinction in Oregon.

Discover BestPossible Living

This all speaks to the importance of the roles the psychology of self-esteem plays in our lives. It is here where we place value on ourselves so that we can value things, time, family and friends, and life itself.

Psychology of Optimism

Our anticipations, expectations, and mental images regarding future events trigger a complex array of physiological, psychological, and social consequences. How we think about the future affects not only our decision making and resulting actions but both our mental and physical health. If we focus mainly on the dark side, we inadvertently create negative consequences; whereas if we visualize and expect good things to happen, we help them become our realities.

For example, before buying a car, you first think about what you can afford to pay to narrow your choices of what make, model, and color you would like to own. As you visualize driving your dream car, you start noticing cars like it wherever you go. When you grow comfortable as an owner, you create the circumstances that allow you to find and purchase your new or used car. If you had been a pessimist, you would most likely have settled for much less than you could have had.

Optimism about your future is needed to make your plans unfold as desired; optimism greatly influences the chances of enjoying favorable outcomes for most of life's endeavors.

Clearly the psychology of optimism deserves much respect en route to BestPossible.

Ambient Happiness

Ambiance and *ambient* are closely related words, and they both have to do with our surroundings. My wife and I have a wonderful, small backyard with a variety of trees, a colorful array of beautiful seasonal flowers, a raised vegetable garden, and wildlife ranging from squirrels and chipmunks to a wide range of birds and butterflies. From the first warmth of spring to the cool breezes of fall, the ambiance of our private sanctuary is our almost-daily getaway for reading, relaxing, and enjoying a flow of gifts of nature. From our backyard living experience, we both elevate our inner happiness to levels that are at the same time quieting and energizing.

The psychology of happiness ties closely to a person's philosophy, optimism, and self-esteem. Happiness is mostly self-created, making it an important aspect of your masterpiece. A person's state of mind is, at any point in time, the psychological state of his or her cognitive processes as affected by thoughts and feelings.

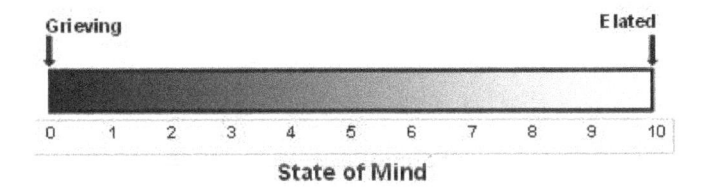

Grieving ↓   Elated ↓

0   1   2   3   4   5   6   7   8   9   10

State of Mind

Discover BestPossible Living

In nature there is a phenomenon called homeostasis that protects our health and lives. It explains how body temperatures hold, like magic, at or near 98.6 degrees Fahrenheit. Through nature-based homeostasis, when your body starts to get too cold, you shiver to warm back up to the healthy ambient 98.6 temperature. Similarly, when you get too hot, you produce sweat that evaporates to cool you down.

Each of us has a unique psychological makeup that works to keep our ambient (average) level of happiness within our comfort zone—for better or worse. At any moment our levels of happiness can vary from zero to ten on our state-of-mind continuum, but it will normally stay close to a level that reflects our quality of life. If we are a dependably happy person comfortable in our own skin, our ambient happiness level will range between six and seven on the state-of-mind scale. If we are an unhappy, pessimistic person, our ambient level may hover at four or lower.

Please note that around a person's average happiness are peaks and valleys. Typically happy people have more and higher peaks and they have fewer and shallower valleys. This is what makes their ambient levels high. There is more to a person's state-of-mind position than a simple number can reveal. Happy people have many nonobvious advantages.

Like all emotions, happiness radiates from your inner self; therefore, that's where your ambiance resides. But unlike our physiological hemostasis, our levels of ambient happiness vary greatly among people according to how they have created

Part Two-The Nature of Self-Creation

themselves. Discovering and practicing BestPossible living is largely about elevating your level of ambient happiness.

Your Moral Compass

The fact that you are a functioning human being is empirical proof that you have a philosophy. You have a concept of reality, you accept as true the information you use to make decisions, and you get along with others. These things show you hold a functioning philosophy.

Because we are a gregarious species, beyond survival the most important role of our philosophies is in setting the stage for interacting with other people within our societies. To determine our interactions, the end product of one's philosophy is what some aptly call one's moral compass.

The magnetic compass was invented more than two thousand years ago. Without this navigation tool, we would be living in a much less-developed world. Today we have GPS technology to tell us where we are physically, but we still need ways to guide us through the complexities and dangers of our social lives.

Your philosophy is your social and moral guidance system. It works to help you make decisions, choose careers and relationships, and perform all other functions of your freewill as related to other people and your local and extended communities. I use the word *help* here because you can intentionally

Discover BestPossible Living

and inadvertently act against your own values by openly or subconsciously following unintended philosophies. You can act contrary to your personal code of ethics; you can choose not to be guided by your moral compass and instead follow the lead of others. I point this out not as discouragement but to help alert you to stay on guard. Your compass's reliability depends on how you constructed it and on your integrity.

Here I have an all too common example from personal experience. Before I became a student of philosophy, I was intrigued and even lured by concepts and visualizations of Utopia—a perfect society designed to be free of problems and injustices. My life could have been literally ruined had I not discovered the flaws and dangers of my unintended, ignorant acceptance of Utopian philosophy. The concepts and dreams of Utopia are totally anti-nature. They deny reality, ignore truth, disregard any need for ethics, and promote the worst of political power and control. Nature is all about survival and advancement. Her incentive and reward systems require challenges and successes. Without problems to solve and injustices to correct, there would be no source of self-esteem, no earned pleasure, no reason to celebrate, and no reason to live. In short, If Utopia could exist, it would soon self-destruct. Utopia is the direct opposite of BestPossible living.

For BestPossible living we need to carefully maintain and use nature-based guidance systems. This ability will be realized with continual development and deliberate use of your gift of cognition.

Chapter 9

Your Spiritual and Physical Selves

We all simultaneously reside within two worlds. We live in our own inner spiritual world and our outer physical world.

Our inner selves, or souls, are elusive; they seem to reside somewhere in our heads within the complexities of our brains, but they may occupy our entire beings. Our spiritual selves use our physical selves to interact in our shared physical universe as we experience love and joy, pleasure and suffering, and all other kinds of emotion.

Our spiritual selves are our command-and-control centers for freewill living—for following our moral compasses as we navigate through the days and years of our lives.

Your essence is your spiritual self; it directs your choices and actions. Your spiritual self chooses how you interact with

Discover BestPossible Living

your outside world. In the context of this book, the more clearly you understand and remember this fact, the better you will be at BestPossible living.

As you will learn in chapter 12, life management is an enterprise where you act as CEO. Your spiritual self is your headquarters, where you decide purposes, plan missions, and lead the activities of your physical self as you venture into your outside world to do what you have decided to do. As CEO you work within your chosen playing field to shape things and circumstances for BestPossible living.

Your Spiritual Self

There is a 2005 movie called *What the Bleep Do We Know!?* It stars Marlee Matlin along with an impressive cast of renowned experts. In an entertaining but serious way, the movie explores the mysteries of how our brains and our inner selves work to process information, make decisions, and create emotions. It leaves its viewers with helpful insights and many unanswered questions. Mostly viewers come away with greater appreciation of the complexities and marvels of how our spiritual selves use our physical selves to interact with the world around us. (If you have not seen this highly rated film, I recommend you put it at the top of your watch list.)

As miraculously fascinating as the human brain is in all it does, how it houses, maintains, and manages our spiritual lives and souls is almost beyond belief. Yet as the master of your destiny, with a few deliberately applied tools, skills, and

Part Two—The Nature of Self-Creation

disciplines, you can do very well at planning, managing, and living a successful, enjoyable life if you do the following:

* Accept the nature of reality.
* Work toward well-defined, wholesome purposes.
* Rely on reason to direct important actions.
* Use your emotions as feedback and incentives for successful action.
* Follow your moral compass with integrity.
* Remain optimistic with expectations of success.

Living by this short list will do wonders. Your spiritual self will take over to reward your successes and to give you flash warnings when you start to get off track.

We can maintain control of our spiritual lives, or we can selectively abdicate our responsibilities to others.

Secondhand living is a trap that comes directly from human nature. Because we want and need to be liked and endorsed by others, it is easy to be sucked into doing what our would-be friends are doing—to go along with their values rather than following our own moral compasses. To avoid such traps calls for careful vetting of all existing and potential friends. If their basic values are not aligned with yours, they probably never will be, and you have no basis for a healthy friendship. Your integrity is far more important and valuable than their pats on the back. Friendships have to work both ways; if there is a misalignment of basic values, it applies to both parties. This is a time to question motives and agendas and stand clear of being used for causes you don't support. Secondhand living is a common affliction to be avoided by all who aspire to do well in life.

Your Physical Self

Today's automobiles are amazing in what they can do. But they serve no purpose parked in garages. However, when properly fueled and maintained and skillfully operated, they serve their drivers' purposes safely and efficiently. Our bodies are like that. When nutritiously fueled and properly maintained, we can reliably use them to act in service to our purposes. The more skillful our inner selves become as drivers and the more clearly we define our intentions, the better our physical selves will perform along our life journeys.

Your inner self connects with your physical self in order to pursue your purposes within the material world. (Recognized or not, everything you do, you do with purpose.) Our conscious selves call on our nature-endowed tool kits to interface with our physical worlds. Our physical selves have four basic functions that serve the freewill nature of our inner world:

* **Perception**—Our five senses (touch, vision, hearing, smell, and taste) allow us to perceive what's going on around us.
* **Location**—Our nervous systems and brains are able to tell us where we are and maintain and adjust our position

Part Two-The Nature of Self-Creation

in the space around us. They let us stay balanced and in control as we move our limbs and bodies. They perform these vital functions through signals from the vestibular function of our ears, the vision of our eyes, and the proprioceptors of our muscles.

* **Locomotion**—We have the power and ability to move ourselves and objects. Whether it is relocating ourselves or moving our extremities to perform tasks, this natural ability is essential to our freedom and independence.
* **Action**—Our physical selves and their natural abilities enable us to pursue our purposes and achieve the goals of our inner selves.

The more clearly you understand what you are doing and why and the more deliberately you go after your objectives, the better your physical body will serve you, and the more certain and rewarding your results will be. This applies to all pursuits, from simple tasks to achieving your most ambitious lifetime goals. For BestPossible living, defining purpose and goal setting rank near the top of vital skill sets.

Naturally Free and Independent

In chapter 1, I observed that all life forms are naturally equipped to live BestPossible lives. For us humans it's our spiritual-physical nature that makes optimal living possible.

Discover BestPossible Living

We are born to live by freewill, and it is by freewill that we direct our physical selves through our external worlds. This means we were born to be free and independent in our choices and actions. It is up to us to learn how to choose and act wisely.

We all naturally learn from birth to call on our conscious minds and tool kits as our primary means of survival. With our pace of development depending on our social environment, we quite naturally become more skilled in cognition and creativity as we grow in years and knowledge. Here's a key point: our pace of learning and skill development is largely up to us.

Recognized or not, everything we do throughout our days is the result of someone's creativity. BestPossible living requires you to be the primary creator in your use of time. Our spiritual selves are remarkably creative. Starting with unlimited imagination, they can do wonders in bringing happiness and prosperity to ourselves and others around us.

BestPossible living requires self-control in the sense that we must consciously choose our own purposes and act accordingly. With every moment of every day, we advance in time. If we are to advance in a direction we want to go, we must be careful in our choices of actions. This is how we gain and enjoy freedom and independence for both our spiritual and physical selves within our inner and outer worlds.

Chapter 10

Your Rational and Emotional Selves

Reason is our basic tool for advancement. It keeps us grounded in reality. Our emotions tell us how we're doing and reward our successes.

George Hayward Joyce defined logic as the science that directs the operations of the mind in the attainment of truth. Survival and advancement require truth. If you are to do well in life, you need to distinguish between reality and fantasy, right and wrong, good and evil. It's the logical you who must make these distinctions. The more you practice and learn, the better you'll become at calling on logic to safeguard your life journeys. In contrast, your emotions record the effects of what you choose to do along the way.

Joint Roles of Reason and Emotions

As covered in chapter 5, reason is our primary tool for making decisions and managing our lives. Reason is the power of our minds that we use to think, to understand, to judge, and to decide alternative courses of action. While reasoning we use logical processes that call on remembered lessons, known facts, and cognition to assess the consequences of choices. We would be hard pressed to overstate the importance of the roles reasoning plays in our lives.

Reason plays many roles in keeping us out of trouble and on safe ground. We use our reasoning power to discern what is true and what is not, to stay grounded in reality, and to make small and big decisions as we navigate through life.

Emotions play equally important roles. They are mental, spiritual, and physical effects of value-directed thoughts and actions. Emotions keep us alive and make us want to stay that way. They reward good behavior and punish bad. They instantly create fear in response to danger. They reconfirm our love of life and will to live. Emotions tell us when we are on track with our values and when to steer away from trouble. Feelings of inner joy, peace, prosperity, happiness, and fulfillment are Mother Nature's emotional rewards of advancement toward BestPossible.

Emotional/Physical Feedback

The role of reason is to guide our use of freewill; the role of emotions is to register results of actions. These two mental roles have a cause-and-effect relationship: in alignment with nature, reason is the cause; emotion is the effect. When we reverse the two and let emotion be the cause and action the effect, we make ourselves vulnerable but not necessarily wrong. If we act to repeat the pleasure of a recent purchase of a chocolate ice-cream cone, the result is likely to be reliably good. It's with complex, new issues that it is better and safer not to act based on emotion.

All forms of action lead to both emotional and physical feedback. We feel happiness throughout our bodies. Happy laughter and tears of joy are natural phenomena that say, "Let's have more!" On the other hand, fear of an approaching storm causes flows of adrenaline that we feel as emotional anxiety and a physical-surge call for responsive action.

Value Judgments

Emotional feedback plays an essential role when we initiate actions on our own behalf. When we act on purpose, as we always do, our goals are set based on prior value judgments. As we act in pursuit of our purpose, the feedback we get tells us how we are doing relative to our related values. This makes what we choose to value of critical importance. If we choose poorly, our emotional feedback will steer us by varying degrees into harm's way.

Value-Based Emotions

At thirty-eight thousand feet somewhere above Utah, I was returning to Seattle from a business trip to New Orleans.

Discover BestPossible Living

I was in deep thought as I reminisced about an encounter I had that afternoon in a Bourbon Street craft shop. While browsing down an aisle, a wood carving brought me to a jolting stop. I was instantly mesmerized. I gently picked it up and marveled at the artistic lines and smooth oiled finish of this beautifully transformed and obviously carefully selected piece of cypress. After seeing its $350 price tag (out of reach for a recent graduate and father of three), I lingered awhile before moving on. Now on my way home and trying to figure out what had happened to me in that gift shop, I found answers that serve me well to this day.

That fifteen-inch carving gracefully captured a beautifully proportioned woman as she was launching from a springboard into a swan dive. Its artist had molded into one piece of wood purpose, self-confidence, grace, femininity, self-control, certainty, and other values I had long held dear. Through his art this man's values spoke loudly and clearly to me and, in doing so, endorsed important parts of my view of life.

This was a great lesson for me. From that day on, I've held a greater appreciation of the role of art in our lives. Contrary to the idea that logic is cold, I learned that understanding why you like something makes you like it better. I recommend the next time you enjoy or dislike a work of art that you ask yourself why. Dig deep for the answer. Most artists are benevolent people with wholesome views of life, and their work will always be enjoyed by like-minded people. The more clearly we see the values of an artist, the more deeply we can appreciate his or her work.

Part Two—The Nature of Self-Creation

To understand your emotions is to intensify them. Understanding emotions makes them close friends, not casual acquaintances. Just as knowing clearly why you love a person deepens your love, understanding the sources of other emotions adds to their intensity and to the roles they play in our lives.

Rational Freewill

The best way to avoid nature-based traps is to stay on purpose and apply common-sense reasoning when making decisions pertaining to major commitments of time and resources.

Given that we are born to live by freewill, we should make the most of this blessing by doing the best we can to always choose values, purposes, actions, and relationships that consistently bring us the rewards of success while keeping far away from harm's way. This calls for what we can call rational freewill.

Emotional results of rational living will always be rewarding and protective. They will give us maximum inner joy, happiness, and feelings of fulfillment while warning of trouble and danger. This is a good rule of thumb to remember: reason-based emotions are healthy; emotion-based actions make us vulnerable.

Chapter 11

Your Social Self

Social and resulting personal relationships are our best sources of happiness and fulfillment.

We all came into this world as pure moral creatures. At birth we needed emotional and physical nourishment for survival and advancement toward independence. Although not so clearly recognized, the same needs extend throughout our lives. To discover BestPossible living and enjoy all it offers, we must rediscover our moral selves and relearn the joys of living in harmony with others and with nature.

Gregarious Living

Being gregarious is part of our nature. We are naturally sociable; we seek and enjoy the company of others, so interacting with fellow humans is an essential part of BestPossible living. In fact this is one of our greatest sources of pleasure and meaningful achievements.

We can only do so much in service to ourselves before we have to tap into our profit imperatives through providing service to others. Beyond this practical consideration, we have needs for love, endorsement, and help that can come only from personal relationships and community involvements.

Natural Morality

The basics of nature-based morality are the surest, safest, and best ingredients for our personal moral foundations. There can be no others that effectively address the issues of right versus wrong, good versus evil, and love versus hate. Promoting one's own welfare requires clear answers to these critically important issues—answers that can come from references to nature. Just as important as the answers is our adherence. Here nature will play her role, like it or not; she will reward our commitments to what's right and good, just as she will discourage and punish things we do that are wrong and evil.

Below is another shades-of-gray continuum. Think of this as a decision continuum. We make decisions with objectives in mind, and how well those objectives get served determines the quality of the decision. *Wrong* means the decision could not be worse: it would be dead wrong. Similarly, *right* means it could not be better: it's the BestPossible choice given our alternatives and circumstances. In between are decisions that would yield mixed results—some favorable, some not. Here it is important to note that shades-of-gray decisions result in avoidable detrimental compromises. If there is no way to avoid compromise, the right decision will be the one offering the BestPossible compromise.

```
Wrong                                              Right
  ↓                                                  ↓
  ┌──────────────────────────────────────────────────┐
  │              Degrees of Workable                 │
  └──────────────────────────────────────────────────┘
                  Decision Continuum
```

The more complex our decision, the greater the distance between the dark and bright ends of its continuum, and the wider and foggier its shades of gray. It's hard to tell which way we're moving in the fog—or if we're moving at all. Because our most important decisions are usually complex, our present positions tend to be a long way from BestPossible.

Good and Evil

What are noble objectives when making decisions? The answer is found within the laws of nature and the nature of wholesome goals and action. Anything that promotes life is wholesome; anything that detracts from or destroys life acts against nature. In the absence of life, there is no issue of morality. These facts of nature explain the basic difference between right and wrong, between good and evil. Good people do wrong things by mistake or out of ignorance; evil people knowingly do bad things on purpose.

Whether by ignorance or deliberate intent, Mother Nature rewards good choices and actions while she discourages and punishes bad and evil actions with setbacks and failures. Because BestPossible is wholesome by definition (see chapter 2), its pursuit is always in tune with the laws of nature. Conversely, acting against nature is never a good idea; sooner or later nature will have her way.

Ignorance is at the root of evil for both perpetrators and their victims. Few evil people think of themselves as evil. This is often due to a paradox of human nature—a natural trap. That is, the smarter we are, the more able we are to rationalize bad behavior. A common example of this is letting one's ends justify one's means. Out of ignorance this leads otherwise good people to follow unwholesome pursuits, to initiate and support the causes of tyrants.

This is an uncomfortable but essential subject if we are to protect ourselves from the dark side of human nature. Evil people routinely do bad things on purpose. They use good-sounding ends to justify indefensible means. Unfortunately, evil people too often find their way into positions of political power where they can gain control of masses of gullible followers.

Our history is littered with the death and destruction caused by evil tyrants. Most notable in recent history are the hundreds of millions of lives lost in the twentieth century

Part Two-The Nature of Self-Creation

under the tyrannical rules of Lenin, Stalin, Hitler, Tojo, Mussolini, Mao Tse-tung, Pol Pot, and others.

Love and Hate

Love and hate are polar-opposite emotions. Love is pro-nature; hate is anti-nature. Love is healthy; hate harms health. Love breeds love; hate breeds hate. Love celebrates life; hate works against life. Given these truths, it is hard to understand why some people choose to hate others and harbor hateful emotions. We find a clue in the fact that much of their hate is directed at people they don't know and at causes they have not studied. Again, ignorance is at the roots of evil.

Emotions are tied to value judgments. One can distrust, but not hate, strangers when there are no opportunities for value judgments. So where does such hate come from? In chapter 3 I listed secondhand living as a trap born of the free-will of human nature. Secondhand people are guided by the values of those they follow (for approval) rather than by values from their own firsthand judgments. Living with counterfeit hate is just as bad as living with self-authored hate because the irrational emotional commitments are just as intense or more so.

People living on the bright side of life know to stay clear of hate and hateful people. They live firsthand according to their own heartfelt values.

Common Sense

Natural morality tends to come from common sense. This is because of lessons we learned as infants and adolescents about survival and success. When close to nature, we learn a lot about reality. Natural morality is tied directly to reality and the laws of nature.

Natural Relationships

There are natural, forced, and mixed relationships among families and friends and within communities, churches, places of employment, and other gatherings of people. In all cases, natural relationships are most comfortable and rewarding because they come from shared values, purposes, and missions.

Forced relationships are uncomfortable because they are unnatural and because they are often conflicting in one or more ways. For BestPossible living and mutually rewarding associations, we must seek to develop friends and find associates where stress-free, win-win situations are likely to prevail.

Your Civic Self

We are all citizens of local, regional, and national communities that are within our sphere of activities and influence.

The world is perceived and experienced individually. This means everyone's world is different according to his or her core values, purposes, perceptions, and expectations.

Part Two-The Nature of Self-Creation

Everyone has an inner personal world within his or her direct control and a societal world within his or her sphere of influence. Perhaps surprisingly the latter extends worldwide. For example, I once read that a feather falling in Tokyo will minutely affect air currents in San Francisco—that no part of our global climate system happens in isolation.

The same is true for each of us as players on the world stage. Others may not notice our effects, but they are real nonetheless. Everyone makes a difference, recognized or not. When we go to work, we add to the economies of our community, our nation, and our world. When we do good deeds and serve others, we make the world a better place. The same is true when we live wholesomely, set good examples, and support like-minded regional and national leaders.

Nature of Compassion

Good people find happiness in making other good people happy. Pursuit of happiness is a key part of human nature, and perhaps the greatest source of happiness is found in helping others and making them happy. This means those who choose to live on the bright side are naturally charitable. In a BestPossible world, charitable giving would be voluntary (instead of through taxation) and close enough to home for givers to know the needs and worthiness of their beneficiaries.

Just before Christmas of 1963, I took my five-year-old daughter, Linda, for an evening shopping trip to Seattle's Aurora Village shopping center. Her mission was to buy gifts for her mother, sister, and little brother. As we climbed the wide steps to the mall's north entrance, Linda let go of my hand to pick up a penny from a dusting of fresh snow. "Look what I found, Dad! Can I keep it?"

She switched her penny from one warmly moist hand to the other as she did her shopping. As we were leaving the mall, her face lit up with excitement: "Look, Dad! My penny turned all shiny."

Out in the cold, Linda stopped again. She was looking through the lightly falling snow at a uniformed Salvation Army woman with her holiday handbell and collection kettle. "I'm going to give my penny." Without hesitation she went over, smiled up at the woman, and excitedly looked into the kettle as she deposited her precious contribution.

Linda's act was not a sacrifice; she had gladly traded her shiny penny for the priceless joy she found in helping poor families at Christmastime. Her glowing happiness came from her wholesome motive and caring action.

Let's look at another situation. Imagine a man walking back from lunch with his boss. He stops to put a ten-dollar bill in a Salvation Army kettle. Let's explore possible motives:

1. He wants to impress his boss.
2. He feels a tinge of guilt for being rich.
3. Because of cultural pressures, he feels intimidated and obligated to donate.
4. He knows of the Salvation Army's mission and will gain much more than ten dollars' worth of pleasure in helping their cause.

Part Two-The Nature of Self-Creation

Of these four motives, only the last is wholesomely in tune with nature. The first is deceptive, while the other two would have been unhealthy submissions to the expectations of imagined others.

Exchanges of value for equal or greater value are what make life work. Just as nature made us gregarious, we are naturally compassionate. In fact, compassion is one of our deepest and most rewarding emotions. Think about how your whole body feels overcome with joy—including tears of happiness—at the end of a touching movie or novel.

Like all emotions, compassion stems from value judgments. Our natural love and respect for life extends to all worthy beings. Who doesn't feel love and joy watching kittens play or when watching a child's first steps? Such events remind us that life is good and wholesome living is possible and worthy of our efforts.

Generous giving based on informed, heartfelt compassion brings the natural rewards of honoring and promoting life. Here firsthand value judgments based on personal knowledge are prerequisites to heartfelt compassion. Because only individuals can make value judgments and have hearts, only we as individuals can know the joys and pleasures of being compassionately generous.

Chapter 12

Your Enterprising Self

*Your life is an enterprise of many purposes.
You play all roles, from CEO to janitor.*

An entrepreneur plans and manages an enterprise. An enterprise is a complex undertaking involving considerable risk. By these definitions everyone's life is an enterprise, and we're all entrepreneurs with the complex, risky task of ever-challenging life management.

Entrepreneurial Start-Ups

With every job change or new initiative, we start a fresh entrepreneurial venture and open an untouched field of opportunity. I've had many different jobs in my life, all successful; each served its purpose very well. From my time as an eight-year-old World War II shoeshine boy to my latest career as a nonfiction author, I've viewed every new job, educational undertaking, and career as an exciting adventure.

Every start-up offers new challenges and rewards. As creatures of freewill, we are naturally equipped to be in charge of each of our enterprises—each of our complicated, risk-prone adventures.

Modes of Life Management

Epicurus, the ancient Greek philosopher, noted that the motives of human activities are either to seek pleasure or to avoid pain. In doing business this translates into either offensive or defensive strategies, tactics, and actions.

We have natural abilities and acquired skills for planning and doing. In most cases we are born with brains adept at creative planning and systematic execution. We use the right hemispheres of our brains to create and our more ordered, analytical left hemispheres to direct systematic actions. These binary functions of our brains are the rudimentary methods of human performance.

How we combine our motives and methods determines how we plan, manage, and live our lives. Our motives and methods greatly affect the outcomes of our efforts.

Our motives tend to migrate between offensive and defensive; at times we work proactively on offense, and at other times we react defensively. Whatever our motives, our methods are either creative (right brain) or systematic (left brain).

Part Two-The Nature of Self-Creation

Superimposing motives and methods, we get quadrants representing four basic modes of action:

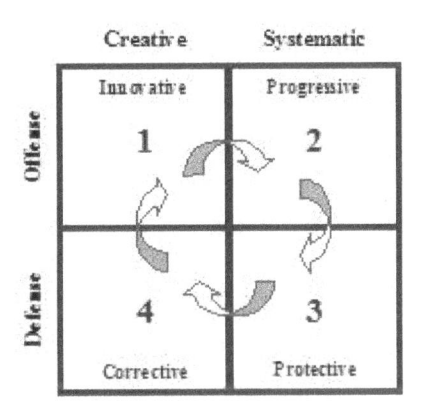

```
                Creative      Systematic
              ┌─────────────┬─────────────┐
              │ Innovative  │ Progressive │
         Offense│     1       │     2       │
              │             │             │
              ├─────────────┼─────────────┤
         Defense│     4       │     3       │
              │             │             │
              │ Corrective  │ Protective  │
              └─────────────┴─────────────┘
```

Leading your personal enterprise is both an art and a science. Creating plans is an art while putting those plans to work calls for science-based disciplines. We need to be both creative and systematic to advance our levels of success.

Whatever our current endeavor, we begin in the innovative mode (offensively creative) to develop plans. We then naturally move into the progressive mode, in which we systematically put our plans into action. At some point we slip quietly and unintentionally into the protective mode (systematically defensive), in which we protect our successes and stay with what we know works. Mode three becomes a comfort zone in which we establish and follow traditions.

When circumstances create a crisis, that puts us into the damage-control, or problem-solving, corrective mode, in which we again work creatively to recover. Successful mode-four activities may stabilize things and buy time to get back to mode three'. However, the most successful approach to crises often is to shift back into mode one, rethink our strategies, and develop new plans.

This clockwise movement through these four universal modes of action is the root cause of many shortfalls in achievements, and this weakness comes directly from human nature. The clockwise movement is also perpetuated by overdependence on traditions that are mainly for defense. Without knowing a safe path for advancement, our natural tendencies are to seek mode-three refuge in the comfort of well-tested traditions.

Although this progression is human nature, we would have fewer self-imposed limitations if we could see beyond the world as we perceive it. We think we are doing the right things in the right ways, or we would be doing different things in different ways. This is much more than an obvious observation; it explains our resistance to change and attraction to comfort zones. Traditions and perceptions are not inherently flawed; in fact, they play vital roles, providing stability and guidance. But as the world changes around us, excessive stability and limited vision trap us on defense and lead us repeatedly into crises. It doesn't have to be that way.

Most commonly we lose ground on defense and move forward on offense. On defense we react to unfolding circumstances. On offense we create plans and systematically execute them. We mold circumstances to better serve our missions.

Part Two-The Nature of Self-Creation

People working toward BestPossible spend their time in the offensive modes of strategy, planning and acting proactively whenever possible and appropriate. They know the more time they spend on offense, the less time and need they have for defense. The best way to avoid losing ground is to stay busy gaining ground. Proactive planning helps ensure purposeful action.

Seeds of success germinate as ideas and take root as plans in innovative mode one. These plans come to life and bear fruit in progressive mode two. Vitality diminishes in protective mode three, and corrective mode four awaits those who fail to cast off outdated traditions. This cycle through the four modes of action feeds on human nature. When we wait too long to act, we are forced to react.

As we systematically execute plans, we gain the knowledge we need to uncover new opportunities and develop fresh ideas. When we stay busy moving back and forth between creative planning and purposeful execution, we minimize the hidden effects of our outdated traditions and their resulting crises.

About Constraints

If we had no constraints in life, we would have no rewarding challenges, no fields of opportunity. Instead of being happy, we would be bored silly. Here I refer to constraints as anything that holds us back as we work to achieve a mission. Ironically, constraints are what allows purpose in our lives.

We have imaginary, self-imposed, and nature-based constraints but no can't-get-there-from-here constraints. With creativity we can find ways beyond any hurdle or impediment. That's what adds adventure, excitement, and rewards to our days and years. Our fields of opportunity are full of constraints—one or more for every opportunity.

Opportunity-Based Life Management

When we think and act creatively and offensively, and we reject the deceptive short-term security of doing business as usual, we are practicing opportunity-based living. This involves systematically tapping into our fields of opportunity. Rather than defending past successes, this is about continually exploring, identifying, and capturing new opportunities.

Our mode-one plans don't deliver value until executed. The more purposefully we put our plans into mode-two action, the more we control our direction and rates of advancement. With purposeful execution, we do what needs to be done here and now to gain from today's opportunities and circumstances.

Selective Service

All our actions are either in service of ourselves or others. The more successful we are in servicing ourselves, the more able and prepared we will be to serve others. This is a definite case of first things first.

Part Two—The Nature of Self-Creation

Serving Ourselves

We have personal needs and responsibilities to care for. Whether it's getting an education, making a living, tending to our health and fitness, building and nurturing relationships, or countless other activities, these things are handled in the context of life management and compete for time with other functions of our personal enterprise. This is important to realize because, as your own CEO, it's important to balance the use of your enterprise's time. Optimal balance will lead to a BestPossible mix of worldly achievements and inner profits.

Serving Others

When you're not serving your own needs and wants, you are working within your personal enterprise to serve others such as friends, family, employees, or others in your community. When you work as an employee or even as a business owner, it is good to realize you are acting by choice as a vendor of services. This is a heathy perspective—to view yourself as always working for yourself and your personal enterprise, which in fact you are.

Fiscal Independence, Spiritual Freedom

Perhaps the essential key to wellbeing and happiness is to have and maintain a healthy self-esteem. When you prove to

Discover BestPossible Living

yourself you are able to take care of yourself while accomplishing significant things, your self-esteem gets a big boost, and you are motivated to be successful as the CEO of your enterprise. Successful life management not only leads to fiscal independence but also builds feelings of self-worth that are essential for inner health and happiness. This makes being an effective, enterprising self an important part of BestPossible living.

Part Three

Your BestPossible Self

Every life endeavor takes place over a journey through time, however short or long.

Liberated living is about deliberately clearing the way so all our journeys are full of adventure and joy. Optimal living may seem to be a daunting endeavor. However, as I hope you have discovered by now, it is not as hard as most would think. First, it is important to remember there's always a way, and it's never too late; there is a way to accomplish BestPossible living whatever your age and situation. The final six chapters of this book cover subjects and offer insights you can use immediately to enhance the quality of your days and the rewards of your various life journeys.

Because you live by freewill, you can determine the destinies of your life journeys. You will learn why this is true and what you can do to make your journeys the best they can be.

Chapter 13

The Magic of Now

Your past, present, and future have much to offer. There is magic in the fact that you can visit and gain from all three dimensions while in your now.

We can look at time in three dimensions: past, present, and future. A marvelous thing about our minds is that we can visit and live in any one of the three whenever we want. Our memories, our awareness, and our imaginations make all three available for use as we work to enhance our lives.

Who we are and how we live in the present is largely a result of the lessons of our pasts. The more we can learn to accentuate past positives and diminish negatives, the brighter will be our present and future.

We derive our present purposes in preparation for our envisioned future. It is by previewing and preliving our plans that we are able to choose and adjust our directions in life.

Discover BestPossible Living

None of this is likely to be new to you; it is part of our nature. We subconsciously call on our pasts as we live and plan our lives. That's why we have memories and creativity. Our abilities to enjoy and gain from three-dimensional time travel are among the most important tools nature provides to help us move toward brightness along our life journeys.

Without what I call "the magic of now," our lives would go nowhere. We call on what we've learned in our pasts to live in our presents and to plan our todays and tomorrows. We naturally and literally use the three dimensions of time to survive and live. How well we learn to do this determines how closely we can approach living BestPossible lives.

To master the magic of now is to consciously use our past, present, and future to lead and enjoy BestPossible lives.

Revisiting Your Past

When you choose to consciously and vividly to go back in time, you will experience past events from more mature perspectives. Because you now have more knowledge and wisdom, you are able to draw fresh lessons by mentally reliving achievements and correcting mistakes.

Because our memories are of the past, our wisdom comes from the past, as do our values. Visits to our past not only let us add wisdom and reconfirm values, they also reinforce past lessons.

One of our most valuable possessions is our self-esteem. All our esteem-building events happened in the

Part Three-Your BestPossible Self

past. By revisiting, reliving, and enjoying past achievements once again, we revitalize their positive influences on our presents and futures.

Time travel into our pasts can help us avoid mistakes and recognize would-be lost opportunities. With broader perspectives of our newer selves, we can internally correct misses and mistakes to gain never-again lessons.

We revisit our past as new, updated people—seeing through new sets of eyes and new value systems. As works in progress, our views are in constant states of change. Revisiting our past is invaluable for optimal decision making. We need to invent our future with BestPossible current wisdom drawn from the past and refined by all we have learned along the way.

Inventing Your Future

Who you will be is dependent on how you view your future. How we see ourselves shapes our futures. What we achieve first appears as images of success. This means we can invent our own futures by visualizing in vivid detail what we want those futures to be. Such inventions are launch pads for planned advancements. Most important among these pictures of success is self-image: we must see ourselves as capable and worthy masters of our destinies.

The best way to predict the future is to shape it to match your visions. Proactive people do just that! There will always be a BestPossible, a way to get there, and good reasons to go for it, for those who want to be the best they can be.

Bowling Alley Mystery

As a high school sophomore, I was invited to join the Future Farmers of America (FFA) bowling team. Although I had never been in a bowling alley, I agreed to fill out their team of five. Our first night, I managed to score a three-game average of 115 and made quite a few strikes—not bad for a greenhorn. I stayed around that evening to watch a men's league play. I marveled at their smoothness and at the scores the best bowlers achieved.

I lived one mile out of town up a gravel road. Walking home under a full moon that night, I used a rounded rock to smoothly deliver imaginary strikes all the way. I repeated this practice several times before our next meet after school on Thursday. My two practice balls were clean strikes, as were my first six frames of actual play. Everyone in the alley stopped to watch my next roll, which produced a 4-6, 7-10 split. I ended the afternoon with a 624 three-game series—a formidable league record—and this was my second time in a bowling alley.

It wasn't until eighteen years later when I read Maxwell Maltz's book *Psycho-Cybernetics* that I came to understand my mysterious bowling achievement. Dr. Maltz explains that our minds don't do well at distinguishing between imagined and real events. He said that when we have succeeded once at a task, our brains know how to control our bodies to succeed again. For a week I had practiced rolling perfect strikes. It wasn't until I was distracted by the watching crowd that I lost touch with my subconscious performance.

Part Three-Your BestPossible Self

The Power of Expectations

Optimism, pessimism, and so-called realism are three classic tendencies that permeate people's expectations for their futures. However unfounded, each has the power to affect how events actually unfold. We watch for what we expect and prepare to devote our mental and physical energy in the direction we expect things to go. If we look for darkness, we see darkness. If we look toward the bright side of life, we see and pursue opportunities. If we stay within the walls of what we perceive to be our realities, we'll not move far from our current comfort zones, whether they're comfortable or not.

Forty-four years after helping FFA's team win its league's championship, I enjoyed a weekend off in Richmond, Virginia, while on a business trip with an employee named Ken. Over Saturday lunch I shared my high school bowling story. Ken quickly said, "Let's go bowling tonight. I want to watch you make eight straight strikes." We both laughed, but we did go bowling that night. I was surprised and pleased to roll a score of 185 after so many years (about thirty) since I had last bowled. Ken teased, "I didn't think you could do it."

Before our next line, I thought about Psycho-Cybernetics and what I'd done and felt so long ago in that eight-lane Paso Robles, California, bowling alley. I stepped up, closed my eyes, and visualized my ball smoothly rolling into the strike pocket. Bingo! A perfect strike! It's hard even for me to believe, but I repeated the process in seven more frames for eight consecutive strikes. I got a spare for my ninth frame and finished with a score of 268—by far my best ever.

Discover BestPossible Living

This was a two-way lesson about the power of expectations. At first I was expecting good, but not outstanding, bowling. Sure enough that's what I got. When I shifted to subconscious control with a confidence from past successes, I entered a zone of natural flow—of noninterference by the limitations and distractions of my conscious self. Reinforced by the many strikes of my earlier game that evening, my subconscious mind knew well how to use my body to roll strikes. I stayed in this flow zone until I started consciously trying hard for a perfect score of three hundred.

I have never thought of that memorable night in Richmond as being about me as much as being about the wonders of human nature and how our mind-body connections work to achieve demanding purposes. This firsthand example says a lot about the powers of expectations and the importance of optimism in the context of BestPossible living.

Psycho-Cybernetics is amazing in how it works and what it can do. For another example, my brother, David is a civil engineer and an ardent golfer. At the time I first read Dr. Maltz's book, David was living in California serving as director of water distribution and flood control for San Luis Obispo County. Not sure how he would relate, I sent him a copy of the book. About six months went by before he called on a Sunday afternoon. Clearly excited he said, "Gene, guess what?" Dave went on to tell his "miracle" story. He had been on his backyard lawn practicing chip shots using about one hundred practice golf balls aiming at a laundry basket. "With two balls left, my shots had formed a scattered pattern around the basket, but none had hit my target. Then I remembered the book you sent me where Maltz says don't consciously try, just vividly visualize the desired outcome. Guess what! My last two balls landed right in the basket."

There are over 650 muscles in our bodies. Whatever action we take, whether it's swinging a golf club or merely walking or talking, there is no way we can consciously control all muscles that are needed for the action. When we try hard to do something with perfection we seldom succeed—perfection is for our subconscious minds.

Law of Attraction

There are ever-active natural laws of our universe that greatly affect our lives. Among these is the law of attraction. Recognition of this law dates back to ancient civilizations. In modern times its powers and effects have been widely studied, observed, and described in various writings. Recently, in Rhonda Byrne's best seller *The Secret*, the author and her many notable contributors cover the law of attraction in considerable detail. The book has been translated into fifty languages and has sold more than twenty million copies. Clearly there is a lot of interest in learning how this natural law can be used to personal advantage.

Actually, most people already gain value without awareness. Optimism versus pessimism, Psycho-Cybernetics, and inventing your future through visualization are common manifestations of nature's law of attraction.

The Buddha said, "All that we are is the result of what we have thought." James Allen's book *As a Man Thinkest* has the same message. We attract our expectations and points of focus. This aspect of the law of attraction is easy to prove and noncontroversial.

For many the law also holds that thoughts generate energy fields that draw to us what we strongly desire and vividly visualize as already being in our possession. This aspect is harder to comprehend, prove, and accept. Either way, we need to learn how to consciously tap into the power of the law of attraction to help make good things happen.

Vivid Visualization

In the many years since the publication of *Psycho-Cybernetics*, many have successfully applied Dr. Maltz's principles to improve how they perform in their daily lives. These principles are widely used in the world of sports, often under the term "the inner game of [you name it]." Many studies have validated the effectiveness of this mental process for self-improvement.

When tapping into the magic of now to visit aspects of your desired future, the more vivid and enjoyable you make your experiences, the more certainly and enjoyably they will become your reality. This is not a theory; it is how human advancement works. Before we buy a shirt, a skirt, a car, or a house, we first visualize ownership and whether or not it fits our expectations and plans. Before we act we have purposes we visualize as improved realities; otherwise, we don't act. This applies to all acts by all people. In this sense we all invent our own futures. But the more skilled, deliberate, and purposeful we are as creative artists, the more rewarding will be our future days and years. That's what discovering BestPossible living is about: discovering how to make your future the best it can really be.

One last point about our futures: the only time we can enjoy them is in the now. When our futures arrive, they arrive as our presents. That means the more vividly we see and enjoy our futures now, the more likely they will unfold as we design them, and the more enjoyable they will be.

Living in the Present

Now is a fleeting, infinitely small slice of time, yet it is all we have to get things done. All our past and recent achievements have been done during strings or periods of time, just as all our future accomplishments will be. This means living in the now is more of a metaphor than a reality. But it's a good, highly useful metaphor. Living in the now is about consciously enjoying and savoring present moments, however long they happen to be.

There is much you can do to enhance and brighten your moments in time. One is to make sure your paradigm fits your abilities, interests, and passions. If this is a new concept for you in this context, we all hold mostly subconscious views of our limits of operations and assumed rules of success. You can think of your paradigm as the fences, map, and rulebook of the playing field for the game you have chosen to play in life.

Reshaping Your Paradigm

Because your paradigm is a map that resides in your conscious and subconscious minds, it is fully malleable. By exercising your freewill, you can change and reshape it any time. The situation of your present paradigm came from your perceptions of what is available and possible. With these perceptions come self-imposed constraints to progress. The surest way to improve your situation and become free of shackles is to broaden your perceptions.

Whatever your paradigm, within its limits are untapped opportunities and rewards waiting to be captured and enjoyed. But BestPossible living includes creatively stretching boundaries and challenging rules to liberate ourselves from overly restrictive perceptions and assumptions.

Typically, working to do better happens mostly inside the box (paradigm), while going for what is truly possible calls for advancements outside the box. This means our greatest opportunities for improvement very likely lie beyond the limits of our present paradigms.

Inventing BestPossible futures is largely about reshaping paradigms. This process calls on our artistic selves. Your paradigms are as malleable as you are creative, flexible, and bold. Adventurous people see change as an ally and reshape their individual paradigms to capture greater opportunities.

Part Three—Your BestPossible Self

Creating Circumstances

James Allen's book *As a Man Thinketh* was first printed in 1903 from a collection of essays that he thought to be too far out for the world of his time. At the urging of his wife Lily, they were published and well received. To this day, the book continues to sell well as an inspirational classic. In this short book of beautifully written prose, Allen convincingly conveys the powerful message that we are creators of our own persons and circumstances.

futures. We have learned a lot since James Allen first shared his wisdom. Many in the world of our time are more than ready to learn about how we create circumstances, how we can do much better at inventing our futures, and how we shape our destinies as we decide what to do.

As we make and carry out plans, we are in fact creating circumstances favorable to our purposes. By proactively pursuing goals, we minimize the distractions of unfavorable circumstances.

Preliving Your Visions

Time exists only in the now. Now is the only time we have to use, but it's a magical time. Besides re-enjoying the best of our pasts, we can prelive our futures even as we live and savor each moment of the here and now.

To live in the present is to be fully conscious of where you are, what you're doing, and why and how your actions are affecting your inner feelings and those of others. This is quite a lot to ask of a minute slice of time. Actually, because that slice is infinitely small, you cannot be conscious of it all at once; such awareness happens sequentially in rapid fire to make our moments alive and rewarding.

We often hear there's no time like the present. These words are usually used to discourage procrastination, but they accurately speak to the remarkable nature of *now*. Our lives involve three dimensions of time. Good use of all three is required for BestPossible living. There is magic in what we call *now*. Everything we do, we do now—even as we reflect on our pasts and enjoy visions of our futures. The magic of now allows us to take full advantage of our pasts, presents, and futures.

Mastering the Magic

My 1942 Fourth of July greased-pole victory has turned out to be a good mini example of mastering the magic of now. (See prologue.) Besides bringing revisited joy into my life, this early conquest has led to a life of can-do accomplishments and to the inventing of a forever-optimistic future.

The Little White Box

Mr. Rodney Wilcox Jones was a master of the magic of now. I was fortunate to see Tom Brokaw interview him in 1983 on NBC's *Today Show*. Unlike the entrances of other guests a camera followed him through the darkened studio over

Part Three-Your BestPossible Self

a tangle of cables. Jones hopped spryly onto the stage and set a small white box on the coffee table in front of Brokaw. Brokaw introduced him as the long-retired chairman and founder of Duofold Inc., the leading manufacturer of thermal undergarments. Brokaw said Mr. Jones was 106 years of age and had an important secret to share.

Mr. Jones said, "What I'm going to say will sound silly to most of your audience, but some out there will understand and gain years from my words: I do not plan to die."

Brokaw quickly said, "Of course you'll die someday."

"I suppose I will, but I certainly don't plan to. Too many put death in their plans and die close to their schedules. Look into this white box; what do you see?"

"It looks like a bunch of moss," Brokaw said.

"You're right, but there's much more. There's a hybrid orchid that will bloom in eight years, and I can hardly wait!"

I was obviously among those who heard his message and have often shared this poignant little-white-box story.

While doing research for this book, I found this quote from Jones, a centenarian who followed his passion into most jungles of the world: "If it weren't for those," said Jones, at age 102—pointing toward nine greenhouses filled with five thousand different varieties of orchids behind his home in New Rochelle, New York—"I'd be dead today."†

† Susan Antilla, "From Underwear to Orchids, 102-Year-Old Rodney Jones Is a Blooming Marvel," People Magazine. December 11, 1978.

Discover BestPossible Living

Sadly, I learned that Rodney Wilcox Jones died in April of 1984, the year following his Tom Brokaw interview. But of one thing I can be sure, he had not planned to die; he too much to do—to live for; he no doubt enjoyed an exciting, adventurous, and rewarding life to the end. He knew how to tap into the magic of now.

Chapter 14

Purposes, Goals, and Waypoints

BestPossible is a universal beacon that lights your way toward any purpose.

Triggered consciously or subconsciously, all that we do we do on purpose. Whether we are working on short-term projects or acting out lifelong journeys, BestPossible results call for clearly defined purposes and vividly visualized, desired outcomes. When we craft those visions to be BestPossibles according our perceptions of what is achievable and desirable, our purposes can be optimally served.

Finding and Serving Purpose

Reverend Rick Warren's *A Purpose Driven Life* is one of the best-selling books of all time. With more than sixty million copies in print and published in more than fifty languages, there is clearly worldwide recognition of the importance of having meaningful purpose. Although this book focuses mainly on faith-based purposes, its premise that we need meaningful purpose to achieve inner spiritual fulfillment holds true for all people.

Because all our actions have purpose, we all live purpose-driven lives. It is of course our choices of what to do with our time and our levels of success that determine how well we live.

No Hurry, Not Critical

Although significant purposes can range from one-day projects to life-journey management, they all provide opportunities to contribute value to our world, to build self-esteem, and to add enjoyment to our lives. The value we deliver to our world through our jobs or careers, relationships, and civic involvement can more than fulfill any needs we may feel to contribute and earn our way through life. These purposes can be very satisfying, even if we never find more noble purposes.

Many never aspire to do great things beyond their normal lives—and that's OK. There is enough meaning in life without having to be rich and famous, make earthshaking contributions, or leave long-remembered legacies. For this reason there is no hurry, and it is not critical that we find notable purposes. Remember, we all lead purpose-driven lives. As

Part Three-Your BestPossible Self

long as your purposes are your own and they lead to a happy, fulfilled life, you can experience the many rewards of your very own BestPossible living.

That said, it is through our long-term and lifetime missions that we can deliver the most value to our world. Including and beyond faith-based purposes, many people would like to find one or more purposes that fit their abilities, opportunities, and passions, through which they can best contribute to their own happiness and to that of others.

So how do we find purpose? "Luck is what happens when preparation meets opportunity." This quote, attributed to early Roman philosopher Seneca, reminds us that we make our own luck. Finding purpose is like that. With preparedness we have a good start, but we have to be ready to recognize unfolding opportunities.

Supersonic Water Jets

Writing this book is a personal example of being prepared to take an opportunity. I was near my 1960 completion of a master's degree in engineering science, for which my curriculum included a mix of structural and mechanical engineering courses. I unexpectedly received a letter from the US Forest Products Laboratory in Madison, Wisconsin, with a fellowship offer. It called for doing wood-machining research at the University of Michigan's School of Natural Resources, a leader in this field. The fellowship's stipend would be enough to fund my planned doctoral studies.

The Madison lab is a branch of the US Forest Service and the US Department of Agriculture. The focus of the study was to find ways to improve utilization of harvests from our national forests. At the time, about 25 percent of harvests were being lost as sawdust and other manufacturing waste.

Backtrack ten years to my summer days on Foster Jordan's wheat farm. One hot evening, a neighboring farmer named John dropped by for a porch visit. Like Foster, he was friendly, cheerful, and healthy, but he had a conspicuous problem: much of his body shook constantly. When I asked about his ailment, he explained how, years earlier, he had unthinkingly put a finger in front of his tractor's diesel-fuel injector to see if it was working. It instantly injected the highly toxic fuel into his blood stream. When I asked why he couldn't see the jet, he said it was not visible but was powerful enough to go through a one-inch pine board without slowing down.

My engineering education and awareness of the power of tiny pressurized liquid jets made my fellowship offer exciting; I was well prepared for this welcomed opportunity. My government sponsors and doctoral committee gave their approval for my proposed research. After building the apparatus necessary to put water under up to sixty thousand pounds per square inch (psi) of pressure, I was able to create 0.003-inch water jets (about the thickness of writing paper) traveling up to five times the speed of sound. After extensive testing of their effectiveness for cutting a variety of wood species and other materials, I wrote, defended, and published my doctoral thesis titled "High Energy Liquid Jets as a New Concept for Wood Machining."

Part Three-Your BestPossible Self

Enterprise Optimization

While in Ann Arbor doing my water-jet research, I had the fortunate opportunity learn about linear programming (LP)—a mathematical method for finding optimal solutions to complex problems. I immediately became fascinated by its potential for taking costly guesswork out of important decisions, particularly in the field of business management. Three years later what I came to call enterprise optimization became a passion. This technology also became the basis for my fifty-year career developing and applying computer-based systems to help companies optimize their operations for BestPossible contributions to their five classes of constituents: communities, customers, suppliers, employees, and owners.

As I describe in chapter 12, by dictionary definition every individual is an enterprise, and the task of life management is much more complex than managing the largest of corporations. This book then is a continuation of my passion and purpose that can be traced back to a wheat farm near Cholame, California. By sharing what I've learned and helping my readers discover and enjoy the art of BestPossible living, I hope to give back significantly for all that Mother Nature and her wonderful world has done for me.

Creating BestPossible Beacons

To achieve BestPossible you need to know what it looks like. Vague targets preclude sharp focus and reliable performance. The best and only way to know what your target looks like is to paint it yourself. Only you know what is right and possible for you. Only you know your ambitions, aspirations, desires, and values. But you are probably asking, "How can I know what my BestPossible is?"

Self-Made Beacons

That's actually a good question. Napoleon Hill's famous quote says, "What the mind can conceive and believe, it can achieve." † I believe this is true wisdom, especially if you vividly visualize your BP before you deem it to be both achievable and believable within the time period being considered.

It doesn't matter if you understate or overstate your potential because just doing better happens on your way to BestPossible. What's important is that you perceive it to be achievable and desirable. Whatever you accept as your targeted BestPossible is sure to improve along your way as you gain experience, skills, and fresher perspectives.

† Napoleon Hill, *Think and Grow Rich*. 1937.

Paths of Least Resistance

While visualizing what is achievable and believable, our minds are also seeing what to do. In this way we visualize BestPossible road maps for getting from where we are to where we can, and would like to, be. In this way we create perceptions of paths of least resistance. As we move forward and get closer to our goals, our best paths become clearer. Just as our BestPossibles become better, so do our road maps.

Waypoints and Mileposts

Long-term goals are journeys that are best traveled by way of notable interim waypoints. For example, if your goal is to earn a college degree, you can deem each of your years of study as a useful waypoint for planning activities and funding. As you progress you can set as mileposts satisfactory completions of required courses. Mileposts even serve well for planning and celebrating midterm and final exams. Defining and visualizing waypoints and mileposts as BestPossibles will help ensure the outcomes you desire. This is not profound; it is how nature and the subconscious work to help us bowl strikes. The better you become at defining and visualizing your BestPossible, the better your score will be.

A Universal Process

This creation and visualization process is universally applicable to all forms of human advancement. We need to see ourselves in our desired futures. Without such images, we have no motivation to change the status quo.

There's magic in going for BestPossible instead of just working to get the job done. By setting out from the beginning toward what you perceive to be BestPossible, it becomes your purpose and mission. By adding well-defined purpose to your actions, you can chart efficient courses, monitor your progress, and make corrections and improvements along the way.

Whether you are working on chores, projects, hobbies, job assignments, career advancement, recreational activities, or waypoints of lifelong missions, if you use this universal process and aim it deliberately at BestPossible beacons, you'll find your outcomes greatly enhanced.

If Farmer John were still alive, he would appreciate knowing his tractor-repair accident had led to the genesis of what is now a worldwide industry: water-jet cutting systems are used extensively for cutting and machining materials of all kinds. Not only that—my visit with John on Foster Jordan's porch that hot summer night led to my enterprise-optimization career and ultimately, my writing of this book.

My story is unique, but it is not that unusual. As is true for most people, my life and career have required reaching for hundreds of waypoints and thousands of mileposts. Everyone has a story in which one thing leads to another. They are all lucky because they create their own luck when they prepare for, recognize, and respond to inevitable opportunities.

Chapter 15

Your Life Journeys

*Each person's life journey is composed
of countless subjourneys, each with
its own challenges and rewards.*

Every person's life journey comes in parts. According to our choices, we travel many parallel and diverse journeys. Nature endows us with freewill and puts us on our own. Along with our freedom to choose comes responsibilities and accountability. We are responsible for the kind of person we decide to be, and we are accountable for the results of our actions. While intending to live wholesomely in tune with nature, it is essential that we honor our responsibilities and hold ourselves accountable for our actions. Our enjoyment and rewards will be greater when we travel with clear consciences.

Joint Travels through Time

Our physical and spiritual selves are distinct but mostly inseparable. They go everywhere together; they travel through time as a joint entity. Each has its own functions but our inner selves are in charge and enjoy all rewards of success. Our physical bodies follow our inner-self orders and tell us what is going on in the outside world. Our two selves work together to make our lives not only possible but either incredibly exciting and enjoyable or terribly miserable and painful, depending on how well we discover and choose to use them for BestPossible living.

When I say "mostly inseparable," I mean our bodies cannot function without our minds. However, our minds can and routinely do act independent of physical constraints. Here we are free to create, invent, fantasize, dream, and tap the magic of now without restrictions. This is how we learn from our pasts, plan our days, and invent our futures.

Travelers All

We are all on planet Earth hurtling through space and time. We have no choice in this matter, but we all have choices regarding what we do as we move through space and time. As long as we're alive and aware enough to make decisions, our age and physical condition do not matter. Whether you are the picture of health or have a serious affliction, have recently lost a loved one, or have suffered an accident or a natural disaster, you have BestPossible ways to invest your time and

Part Three-Your BestPossible Self

move forward. There is always a way, and it is never too late to reach for your BestPossibles, no matter how bright or dim things seem to be.

This chapter has examples of both worldly and spiritual life journeys. Whatever your physical condition, your inner, spiritual self is free to tap into and enjoy the magic of now to whatever extent is possible.

Journey as a Metaphor

Whether physical or spiritual, the journey metaphor works for any movement beyond where we are toward where we would choose to be. This chapter covers a variety of activities that are common to most of us as we plan and lead our lives. Below you will find correspondingly labeled continuum-based models you can use to estimate your current status for each journey on a zero-to-ten scale.

As you do this, please remember BestPossible is not the same as perfect: it is the level of achievement you perceive is currently possible given your interests, abilities, resources, and priorities. For example, for the friendship continuum, you can give yourself a score of ten with very few but satisfying friends, meaning you have neither interest nor time for more close friends given your current priorities. I strongly recommend you take time to think about and score all continuums. This will give you a rough preview of where you now stand; you may find you're doing a lot better than you realize.

Artwork in Progress

In chapter 7 you learned that your masterpiece is never finished; it is forever in a state of conscious and involuntary change. This is good news. As the artist you are responsible for creating who you choose to be; you can add or cast off whatever you need to as you work toward your latent BestPossible self.

Below are three universal journeys and matching continuum I've included as examples of masterpiece development:

Philosophy is by far the most important dimension of who you choose to be. Your philosophical self sets your stage for staying grounded in reality, gaining valid knowledge, living with wholesome morality, enjoying art, and supporting sound politics.

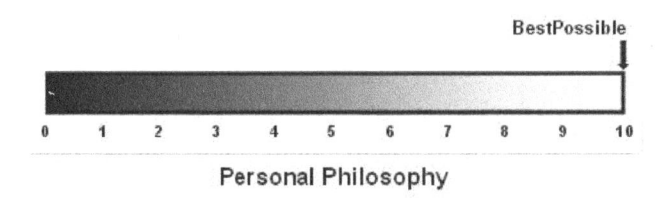

Personal Philosophy

Health determines your physical readiness for life's journeys. Whatever your circumstances, you will always have BestPossible ways to care for yourself. Even people with serious diseases have BestPossible treatment and care options.

Personal Health

Part Three-Your BestPossible Self

Fitness goes hand in hand with health to enable you to carry out your chosen purposes in the physical world. The more fit you are, the more energy, stamina, and productivity you have for demanding endeavors. Strength and fitness minimize limitations to many of your BestPossibles.

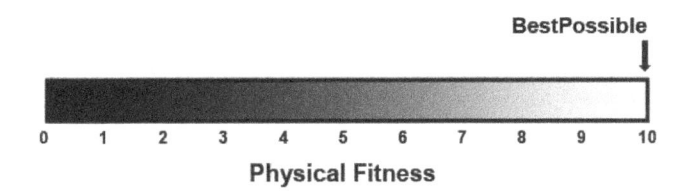

Physical Fitness (scale 0–10, BestPossible marked at 9)

Worldly Journeys

You venture into the physical world to carry out your plans and to interact with others. Because time is limited and precious, it is important that you choose your journeys and supportive actions carefully, based on your freewill and personally embraced values.

Your En Route Enterprise

Education is liberating. It adds to our knowledge, sharpens our skills, broadens our paradigms, expands our perceptions, and multiplies our opportunities. BestPossible education reaches beyond what we need for our work and social lives to include what we need to know to effectively serve whatever purposes we choose to pursue. Because education has many kinds of inner rewards, we can use and enjoy as much as we can get.

Discover BestPossible Living

Education

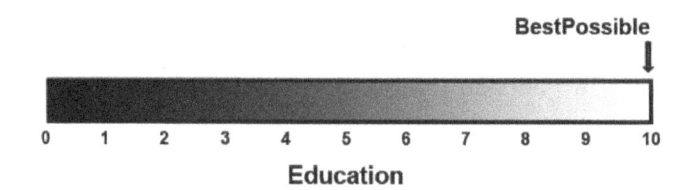

Careers are means to ends, and the best means are those that fit our interests, skills, and passions. They are even better when they also serve noble missions and high purpose. Through our careers we gain the self-esteem, freedom, and self-control we need for BestPossible living.

Career

Material wealth frees us to broaden our fields of opportunity. As we balance our priorities, gaining wealth offers great leverage for making our lives and our world better.

Material Wealth

Recreation is an essential part of life. Besides being a form of celebrating accomplishments, it celebrates the whole of life. It is time for rest and relaxation, reflection, and rejuvenation

Part Three-Your BestPossible Self

for ongoing BestPossible living. The social value of recreation is hard to match when shared with family and friends.

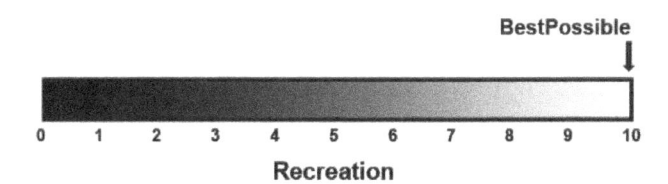

BestPossible ↓
0 1 2 3 4 5 6 7 8 9 10
Recreation

Retirement parties are really commencement celebrations. Just like graduation days, these occasions mark new beginnings. For this, we need new life-sustaining purposes. I like to think of retirement as liberation, a time that marks an increased degree of freedom.

BestPossible ↓
0 1 2 3 4 5 6 7 8 9 10
Retirement

In addition to these universal life endeavors, there are endless personal and shared journeys we travel throughout our lives.

Social Journeys

Social opportunities appear regularly on our worldly journeys. Because social contact is inevitable, it is especially important to stay objective and alert before joining hands for prolonged social involvements. As I covered in chapter 7, sharing of core values forms the foundation for wholesome, mutually rewarding relationships.

Birth and adoptive families play dominant roles during our early years. As we learn to choose and embrace firsthand values and lead our own lives, we create our own character. How close we remain and how much love we give and receive depends on the strength of family ties and the sharing of values and experiences. But whatever the case, our immediate relatives will always have a lot in common for lasting involvement.

New families open whole new worlds to develop, explore, enjoy, and celebrate. Every marriage brings together two extended families along with broadened challenges and hopefully rich rewards for BestPossible living.

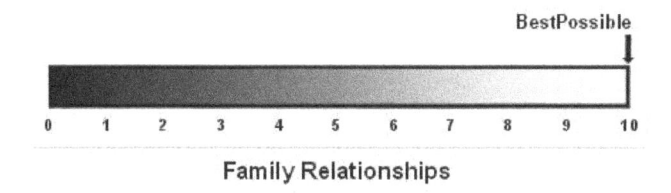

BestPossible ↓
0 1 2 3 4 5 6 7 8 9 10
Family Relationships

Friendships give our lives meaning and high purpose. The more wholesome our relationships, the more peaceful and prosperous our lives will be. Wholesome relationships based on shared values add specialness to our days and years.

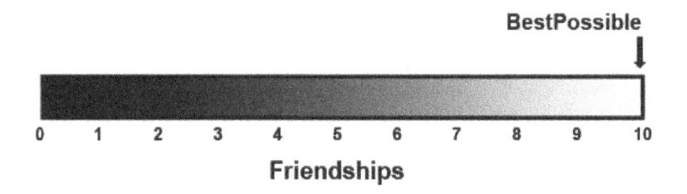

BestPossible ↓
0 1 2 3 4 5 6 7 8 9 10
Friendships

Part Three-Your BestPossible Self

Spiritual faith is an important part of the lives and activities of people all over the world. The time they invest in their faith-based activities helps form their moral compasses, gives them meaningful purpose, and provides answers to critical questions such as, *Where did I come from? Why am I here?* and *What will happen when I die?*

BestPossible ↓

0 1 2 3 4 5 6 7 8 9 10

Spiritual Faith

Inner Journeys

With our worldly journeys come flows of emotions that connect our inner, spiritual selves with all that happens around us. Relationships and possessions provide sources of joy, happiness, and fulfillment. All this happens inside our minds, along our inner journeys, at the cores of our beings.

Inner wealth is a measure of progress toward greater self-worth. It ties closely to performance of good works and win-win relationships. Inner wealth starts and grows with self-esteem.

BestPossible ↓

0 1 2 3 4 5 6 7 8 9 10

Inner Wealth

Inner peace comes with travel toward being more comfortable in one's own skin. Inner peace builds in parallel to inner wealth and its wise use.

Inner Peace

Inner prosperity resides within people of free, creative minds full of ideas on how to make their lives and world better. Prosperous minds continually gain knowledge as they contribute more greatly throughout their spheres of influence.

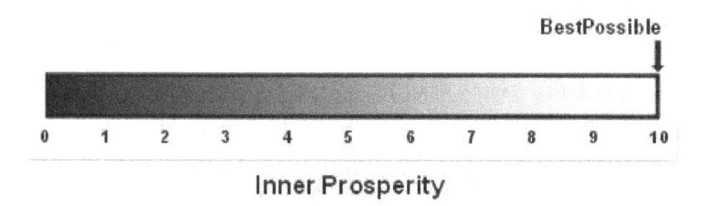

Inner Prosperity

Happiness is a deep-seated state of wellbeing that grows exponentially with successes on our other spiritual journeys.

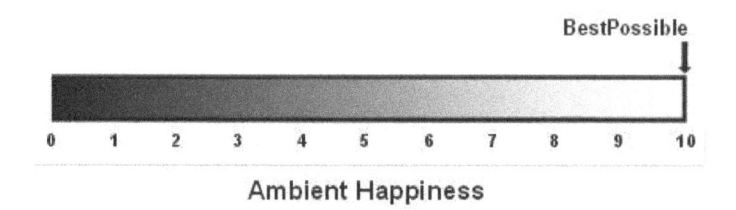

Ambient Happiness

Part Three—Your BestPossible Self

Balancing Your Life

Life balance is necessary for truly BestPossible living. An out-of-balance life can deliver many rewards but at the expense of others. BestPossible balance comes through carefully setting noncontradictory priorities that do not neglect essential involvements while tending to others. An all-too-common example is the workaholic who misses out on needed and more rewarding time with family and friends.

Of all possible continuum, one of the most important for BestPossible living is one that shows how effective you are at optimally balancing all priorities. To score a perfect ten on all your key journeys would be nearly miraculous. But by weighting your individual scores according to your personal priorities, you can use an additional continuum to mark where you are relative to maintaining BestPossible balance among all current purposes and responsibilities. If all you have time for is a score of six on the relationship continuum, and you achieve a six, that score should be recorded as a ten; remember, BestPossible considers all circumstances, including other time demands.

BestPossible ↓

0 1 2 3 4 5 6 7 8 9 10

Life-Balance

Discover BestPossible Living

Quality of Life

Your quality of life is a reflection of the sum of your worldly and spiritual achievements. The ultimate measure is spiritual. Its rewards are the warmth of inner glow, lasting peace of mind, and pervasive happiness.

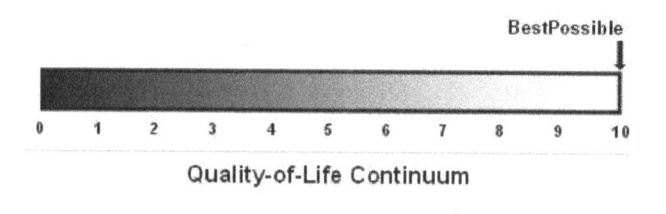

Quality-of-Life Continuum

There are no hard-and-fast constraints on your various BestPossibles. All hurdles and roadblocks will yield to your creativity; you can always get there from here.

Let's take a look at what you can expect as you travel along paths that lead to your BestPossibles. First of all, your life will change in many ways—all for the better. You'll continually gain insights for better use of your freewill. The subtle and not-so-subtle changes you will experience will add incentives to clear your way for steady advancement. Understanding these facts will further enable you to become the master of your destiny for whatever journeys you choose to travel.

Chapter 16

Three Golden Keys

*Keys are for gaining access to something special.
What can be more special than a BestPossible life?*

This chapter briefly covers three natural keys for assured success at BestPossible living. With each key are lessons and insights covered in this book. Even with periodic reviews of the highlights in the appendix, it will be hard for you to recall what's important. Reviewing this short chapter will help bring to mind what is necessary to optimize your days and years.

Reading descriptions of these three keys may again give you the impression that going for a BestPossible life will be a daunting, demanding, and time-consuming undertaking; however, because BestPossible is the natural way to live, it's none of these things.

Going with the flow of nature is following paths of least resistance. With perceiving and visualizing what is possible and best for you come visions of how to make it happen: you see and can then follow least resistant road maps. As for being time consuming, time stops for no one. Making BestPossible use of your time will always be the way to get the most out of your life.

Golden Key One — Be Your BestPossible Self

There will always be ways to make yourself into a better person. That's why going for BestPossible is a journey toward an ever-improving destination. Becoming your BestPossible self is not about arrival: it's about intent and advancement. Proclaiming your sincere, determined intent along with regular progress makes you into your here-and-now BestPossible self. As long as you are truly doing the best you can with what you have, you'll deserve and enjoy the spiritual and material rewards of being the best you can be.

Your Masterpiece

Self-creation is a matter of fact: by your lifetime of choices and actions, you are who you made yourself to be. Your first key to BestPossible living is recreating your masterpiece to be the best it can be according to your current interests, skills, ambitions, and priorities. This is the subject of chapter 7, where you'll find insights that will now help you put its points into today's context.

Part Three-Your BestPossible Self

It is important to note and remember that your masterpiece is a work in progress that can be changed and made over anywhere along your way.

Your Philosophy and Morals

These are essential issues in determining the quality of any person's life, especially those who aspire to live on the bright sides of their continuum. Being firmly in touch with reality is necessary for a nature-based foundation.

A wholesome, philosophical position on the field of ethics will lead you toward morals that thrive on goodness, love, and compassion. Your nature-endowed rights to life, liberty, and the pursuit of happiness are contingent on having morals that honor those rights for all others.

Your Values

Core values of honesty, fairness, justice, and integrity must come before optimal living is achieved. Without these basics, deeply imbedded values, many of your activities will lead to more harm than good. These are nature-based values that are universally shared by all good, wholesome people: they are what lead to peace and prosperity wherever they exist—which they do throughout much of our world.

Beyond your core values you have personal values include cherished relationships, preferred uses of time and money, and current possessions. They come from value judgments.

Discover BestPossible Living

If you like chocolate ice cream better than vanilla, it's because you've sampled both and judged chocolate to be better. Values without experience-based judgments are secondhand, based on the judgments of others. Firsthand living is prerequisite for being your BestPossible self.

Your Enterprise

Chapter 12 explains that your actions are services you provide for yourself and others as products of your personal enterprise. As your own CEO, you manage your life, which offers your greatest challenges and rewards.

BestPossible use of the first key calls for you to plan and use your days and years for well-chosen purposes: those that will yield high levels of inner peace and prosperity along your various life journeys.

Golden Key Two — Live BestPossible Days and Years

To be a BestPossible person is to lead a BestPossible life. It is to plan ahead and wake up each morning with the deliberate intent to make this a BestPossible day. To make each day and every year the best it can be sounds like a New Year's resolution; why would anyone hope for less? The difference is in the degree of resolve one has about making good use of his or her one life to live. When you start enjoying being your BestPossible self, going for BestPossible days and years happens quite naturally; it's a simple matter of acting on your purposes along your life journeys.

Part Three-Your BestPossible Self

Live with Purpose

Everything you do has purpose, consciously recognized or not. The more careful and deliberate you are at choosing purposes and taking supportive actions, the more able you will be to direct your efforts toward what is truly BestPossible.

Mileposts and Waypoints

To go for BestPossible, you first need to know what it looks like. Only you can know this. When you perceive, visualize, and describe in detail what you believe to be a BestPossible milepost or waypoint, you are creating a personally tailored destination BestPossible. Whether or not it is an accurate portrayal is not important. As you head that way, your target is more likely to get better than to prove unachievable.

Tend to Business

While living BestPossible days and years, most of your time will be spent tending to the business of your personal enterprise. (See chapter 12.) Your enterprise is a means of planning and delivering services in exchange for something of value. When you successfully service your own interests and purposes, you do so for expected commensurate material and spiritual gains. You render services for an employer in exchange for paychecks, economic security, and the pleasure of jobs well done. When you service friendships, you gain love, appreciation, and endorsements of self-worth.

This is about the ever-challenging discipline of life management. The better you become at being the CEO of your personal enterprise, the more successful your life journeys will be.

Balance Your Priorities

It's always tempting to service what appears to be the most urgent at the expense of the most important. Health, fitness, education, career, family, and recreation are all important and need their share of your carefully balanced priorities. For BestPossible days and years, this aspect of life management warrants frequent attention.

Continuum

Scaled continuum bars can be used to show history by marking and dating statuses en route. Each mark will of course be a subjective estimate but will nonetheless be helpful for diary or logbook notations.

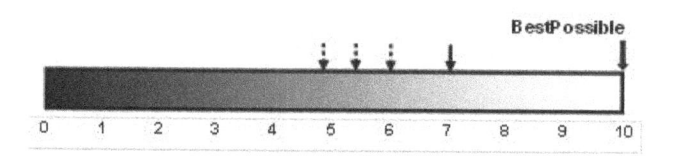

The point here is that, by recording well-described goals and tracking progress, you can make timely adjustments in response to unfolding opportunities and circumstances.

Golden Key Three — Celebrate Your Successes

I love this anonymous quote: "Success is a journey, not a destination." It says so much in so few words. When moving toward honorable goals, every step forward is a success worthy of celebration. While saving shared celebrations for reaching waypoints and milestones, we can and should celebrate every success along our way.

Steps forward and daily achievements are all successes that get rewarded with pleasing moments of reflection and restful sleep. By being consciously aware of these natural pleasures, you can make them into inner mini celebrations that add quiet encouragement.

There will always be many good reasons for BestPossible living. Participants will forever find their inner, spiritual celebrations of life in many forms among the material rewards for their successes.

Along with attendant rewards, celebrations of success provide lasting incentives for continuing success. They also help confirm that our efforts are on track.

Your Golden Key Ring

These three keys are mental concepts for gaining access to a world of spiritual freedom and liberty. They have the power to unlock self-imposed shackles and free us to achieve our true potential in all that we choose to do. We are born to live by freewill with no instruction manual. Although we are born fully equipped to live BestPossible lives, we have

Discover BestPossible Living

to find our own ways through a world of complex challenges and infinite opportunities. By keeping these three keys on a single golden ring, you will have them available to work together as needed to free you for the journey to any preferred BestPossible destination.

Chapter 17

Taking Flight

*To soar with eagles all you need to
do is believe that you can fly.*

—Anthony T. Hinck

To launch the process of BestPossible living is not hard—all it takes is clearly informed intent, determination, and proclamation. To keep it happening will require breaking contrary habits and avoiding backsliding as long as it takes to revel in the rewards of your new life. Once you are solidly on your way, your *Golden Key Three* celebrations will keep you climbing to higher heights with minimal distraction. New determination will soon overcome temptations to move backward.

To handle and overcome inevitable discouraging setbacks, it is good to remember that success is a journey and is not about arrival at a destination. Not all of your steps will be successful and you will make mistakes along the way. But your rewards for success will be more than enough to keep you on a track that qualifies as BestPossible living.

I started my career as a management consultant while a professor in the forestry department at Humboldt State University, Arcata, California. Because I had no Friday classes I was allowed to do outside work. With potential clients all along the west coast into British Columbia, Canada, I learned to fly and bought a small airplane (Piper Cherokee) to get between my clients' mills and computer centers located in Palo Alto, California. I had to do a lot of night and weekend flying but it was workable.

Skilled piloting of airplanes is in many ways analogous to BestPossible living. It involves most of the ingredients and dimensions required for purposeful, skillful and safe life management. Flying always involves well-defined purposes, careful planning, awareness of and heeds to risks and dangers, tending to unfolding circumstances, observance of rules, recognition and honoring laws of nature, codes of ethics, navigation skills, and constant demands for free-will choices.

The Four Forces of Flight

There are four kinds of forces that affect all things that fly. They are:

* **Weight** – This is the force of gravity acting on all system elements such as the airplane itself, its fuel, the pilot and passengers, and all pieces of luggage and other cargo.

* **Lift** – is the force that acts at a right angle to the direction of motion through the air and directly opposite to gravity.
* **Thrust** – is the force that propels aircraft in the direction of their flight.
* **Drag** – is the force that acts opposite to the direction of flight. Drag is a frictional force that increases with relative air velocity (the aircraft's air speed plus headwind or minus tailwind).

Just as these four forces are always there for all birds, butterflies, and pilots, it is helpful to be aware that these same forces come into play throughout our personal lives:

Life's Weight

These are the events, attitudes, people, and circumstances that tend to pull and hold us down. They are tendencies that are all around us every day that gain power from inaction. Perhaps the greatest weight a person can carry is low self-esteem. The certain antidote and remedy to weight is *lift*.

Life's Lift

There are many ways we can create lift in our lives (most are covered in the chapters of this book). In addition to all-important self-esteem, optimism and the power of positive thinking lift spirits, expectations, and levels of achievements.

Love is always uplifting just as hate adds unnecessary weight to our lives.

Life's Thrust

Anything that allows and helps move us forward adds thrust in our lives. Among our best sources of thrusts are: inspired vision; love of life; firsthand values; purpose-focused action; ambition; education; wisdom; freedom; and liberation.

Life's Drag

There are many things we can let be drags on our lives. Because drag is the opposite of thrust, the absence of what allows to advance are the very things that hold us back. They include: ignorance, hatred, envy, secondhand living, dependence and laziness,

Owner's Manual

After buying a Cherokee I almost wore out my owner's handbook studying, learning and memorizing key aspects of my plane's features, capabilities and limitations. I understood how important this was to my own safety, that of my passengers, and my proficiency and reliability as a pilot.

Planning and traveling our life journeys is far more demanding and risky than flying airplanes, and yet we are expected to find our way and stay safe without an owner's manual. Instead we learn to depend on others to show us what life is about and how to make the most of it. While we can do quite well at survival this way, it is likely to lead to a highly compromised journey through life.

As Dr. Albert Einstein observed, Mother Nature is a great and reliable teacher but her lessons don't come in print and are often learned in hard ways. Unfortunately, because nature's lessons can easily remain unrecognized or can be inadvertently and deliberately mistranslated or ignored, we too often stay vulnerable to paying the price of violating nature laws. This all points to the importance of BestPossible living; of doing all we can to find our best ways along life's highway.

Licensed to Fly

I hold three government-issued private pilot licenses. First, I met FAA's (Federal Aviation Administration) requirements to reliably and safely fly single engine fixed wing (not helicopters) aircraft under VFR (visual flight rules). This license allowed me to fly day or night as long as I obeyed all FAA regulations and could see where I was going and what my plane was doing.

My next license allowed me to fly IFR (instrument flight rules). The requirements and testing for IFR certification were highly demanding but once accomplished, I was free to fly through clouds and bad weather with visual references for orientation.

I later moved up to owning and flying twin-engine planes. This required a third license showing that I was qualified and certified to fly multi-engine airplanes under IFR conditions.

Advancements in my licensing were as demanding as they were liberating. And with each came added expectations and responsibilities. Here again my flying metaphor applies well to real life. In our early years and through our youth we have limited responsibilities but we must be able to see where we're going and what we're doing if we are to live safely and stay out of trouble. As we become adults our responsibilities grow and our "flying" becomes more complex, demanding, and unforgiving. Just when we are in greatest need for an owner's manual for answers, our questions become more numerous and serious.

Qualified, Certified, and Diplomas

When my oldest sister graduated from the eighth grade, boy was I impressed. She proudly showed me her diploma that certified she had satisfactory completed all that was to be learned in grammar school and was now qualified to take on high school – pretty heady stuff for a third grader.

Diplomas are like pilot licenses in that they certify that their recipients are qualified to "fly up" to new levels learning and living. Be they for high schools, trade schools, junior colleges, or universities, commencement exercises are just that—the issuing of diplomas mark the launchings of new phases of peoples' lives—lives for which they have been certified to be qualified to begin.

Virtual Licenses

"Qualified to begin" of course doesn't make one an expert or superstar. "To begin" means being ready to gain experience, skills, and wisdom needed to become a truly valuable contributor. With sharply focused attention, study, and action, those working to become their best-possible selves will continue to gain qualifications, promotions, and added responsibilities. These advancements will not come with school-day diplomas but will be certified by self-awarded virtual licenses that speak loud-and-clear about who you are and what you have to offer. As you become increasingly skillful at recognizing and selectively harvesting from your *field of opportunities*, there will be no limit to how high you can fly. Remember, BestPossible will endlessly get better as you get better.

Preflight Checklist

One of the first things I learned about flying was the critical importance of equipment reliability. Besides thorough annual inspections, before taking off I was required to complete a list of preflight inspections. *Golden Key One* as describe above is about getting yourself ready for safe, reliable travel along your various life-journeys. Preflight checklists are important but there is much more required. Because your "plane" is homebuilt you need to make sure it is well constructed, properly maintained, and equipped with the kind of moral compass that will guide you safely through periods of darkness and bad weather.

Again, staying in tune with nature will be your best safeguard against problems, turbulence, and destruction. Because it is possible to choose to be on the right side of these aspects of natural law, anything short will fall short of BestPossible living:

Golden-Key-One Checklist

* **Reality** – Accept reality as real. Observe and honor the laws of nature. Don't try to improve on nature – it can't be done without paying the price of violating natural law.
* **Truth** – What is true is true, independent of perception. Seek to know what is true and choose and act accordingly.
* **Ethics** – There are big differences between good and bad, between right and wrong and they are not subjective. Where there is no life there is no question of morality. Nature promotes life – she says what promotes life is good and right.
* **Morality** – The components of a nature-based moral compass include honesty, fairness, justice, and integrity. To stay in tune with nature is to live by these core values.

Part Three-Your BestPossible Self

Flight Management

The four modes of management concept I described in chapter 12 first came to me from my flying experiences. When I started using it with clients to help them better visualize, integrate, coordinate, and prioritize their four basic areas of management. I was pleased to see how quickly top executives embraced the concept and I soon realized it applies to all human endeavors including the complexities of life management.

This makes my flight metaphor especially appropriate for listing and discussing *Golden Key Two* applications. To live BestPossible days and years is all it takes to become skilled at BestPossible living—a process you must do one step, one day, one year at a time. As pilots fly one mile, one waypoint, and one destination at a time, they gain skills, learn lessons, make adjustments, build memories, and enjoy their successes all along their routes.

Golden-Key-Two Checklist

* **Your Masterpiece** — Remember you are the artist responsible for creating who you are and will be. And remember your masterpiece in and always will be a work-in-process; your free-will will lead to adjustments and even makeovers along your way toward an ever-improving BestPossible.

* **Stay Optimistic** – Expect success in all you choose to do. Visualize brightness; never focus and dwell on the dark sides of life.
* **Magic of Now** – Gain greater wisdom from visits into your past. Invent your future by creating BestPossible beacons to light the way toward who you choose to be; pre-live your "new you" vividly and joyfully. Take plenty of time to live and enjoy your precious present moments.
* **Know Your Philosophy** – Build and live on your own foundation. Don't live by default and secondhand values; be your own person.
* **Moral Compass** – Base yours on nature's code of honesty, fairness, justice, and integrity. Always know the differences between right and wrong, good and evil; strive to be and remain a wholesome, good person—a BestPossible person.

Smooth Landings

Among pilots there is a common joke that says the sure sign of a good pilot is one who has equal numbers of successful takeoffs and landings. Not quite! A good pilot knows how to maintain sure control of his or her machine to make equal numbers of smooth takeoffs and landings. When first learning to fly, I spent many hours at Eureka's Murray Field doing "touch-and-goes" in all kinds of winds and weather. Throughout my thirty-two years of flying I never stopped honing my skills. BestPossible living is like that — the better

Part Three-Your BestPossible Self

you get, the better your BestPossible gets. And your rewards for achievements never stop coming.

Every success en route to BestPossible is a smooth landing worthy of celebration. Celebrations of successes are nature-based rewards that give incentives for more success, for survival, and for the assurance of human advancement. Because they are natural, our inner spiritual rewards come automatically with every achievement. We naturally feel quiet pleasure, satisfaction, and boosts of self-esteem with every success—large or small. But there are things we can and should do to amplify the value of our celebrations.

Golden-Key-Three Checklist

* **Life** – When you celebrate life you are enjoying a lump-sum celebration of all of your successes. This is a prerequisite foundation for BestPossible living. Without a deep-seated love of life you will lack reason and incentive to make your journey the best it can be.
* **Pride** – The deep-seated feelings of pleasure you enjoy are nature-assured celebrations of your achievements. They make you feel proud and ready for more life-promoting activity. Deeply felt inner pride is a wholesome motivator to be quietly enjoyed with the successes of all of your noble endeavors.
* **Prosperity** – With accumulating successes come rising levels of prosperity. These are realized as growing spiritual and

material wealth. When you celebrate achievements, deep down you are enjoying fruits of your productivity and resulting prosperity.

* **Daily** – With each of your self-created daily BestPossible beacons is a ripe field of opportunities to be selectively harvested and enjoyed. When you get up and set out to live a BestPossible day, you'll end the day with the warmth of purposeful accomplishments and ready to celebrate with a nice dinner and a good night's sleep.

* **Waypoints and Milestones** – These are major successes deserving of special recognition and special shared celebrations. They include graduations, promotions, completions of major projects, and other such accomplishments. Their celebrations are important rewards for jobs well done. They make us proud and happy while allowing others to be happy for us as a way of providing encouragement and incentive for continuing success.

Soaring with Eagles

Soaring is in stages, it progresses as you engage in the very art.

—*TemitOpe Ibrahim*

Part Three-Your BestPossible Self

We have learned a lot from eagles and still have a long way to go. These wonderful birds are masters at staying in tune with nature. They can effortlessly soar up to 15,000 feet elevation by instinctively following paths of zero resistance in the form of uplift air currents.

We humans have been watching, marveling, and in our imaginations have been soaring with eagle since we first saw these magnificent birds take flight. Napoleon Hill observed "What the mind can conceive and believe, it can achieve." This has been proven to be true throughout history. Beyond our today's physical air and space travel, our inner spiritual selves are without limits in what we can imagine and achieve.

We can certainly imagine and achieve what we perceive and believe to be best possible. And nobody need be discouraged if they see their BestPossible as not being very good or too far away. If it is not very good right now, it will get continually better as it is successfully and joyfully approached. If it is in fact far away, that means its field of opportunities is expansive and ripe for harvest.

With our gifts of freewill, cognition, thought, and reason we can get the four forces of flight working in our favor to discover and truly enjoy the unending rewards of BestPossible living. And because our most meaningful and lasting rewards come to our inner selves, they lift our spirits to soar with eagles.

Chapter 18

Nature-Based Conclusions

We are all born naturally equipped to lead BestPossible lives. Because we have one life to live, it's important to make it the best it can be.

This final chapter provides nature-based conclusions for added significance and context for this book's many lessons and insights. I believe many readers will find value in periodically visiting this chapter along with Appendix A as they become more skilled at BestPossible living.

BestPossible Living is Natural

By definition you can be your BestPossible self. BestPossible living is not as unusual or rare as you may assume. Nature equips us to live BestPossible lives, but our freewill calls for us to live this way by choice. To do this we have to acquire the necessary skills.

Discover BestPossible Living

It is quite natural for people to live as close as they can to the bright side of their quality-of-life continuum. Of the people in our world today, the vast majority have wholesome moral compasses and wants to prosper and live free, peaceful lives. What I call a BestPossible life is not just possible, but it is nature's intent for all people. There are roughly 7.5 billion people in our world today, and based on a normal-distribution bell curve, the average person lives between 3.5 and 6.5 on the zero-to-ten quality-of-life scale. About 5 percent live within 20 percent of BestPossible. This means about 375 million people are already enjoying close to BestPossible living. This book is offered to help its readers gain the knowledge and develop the skills to join the ranks of those living BestPossible lives if they are not already there.

This first conclusion is perhaps my most important. To lead near-optimal lives, it is helpful to know that, because it is nature's design, millions are already doing it.

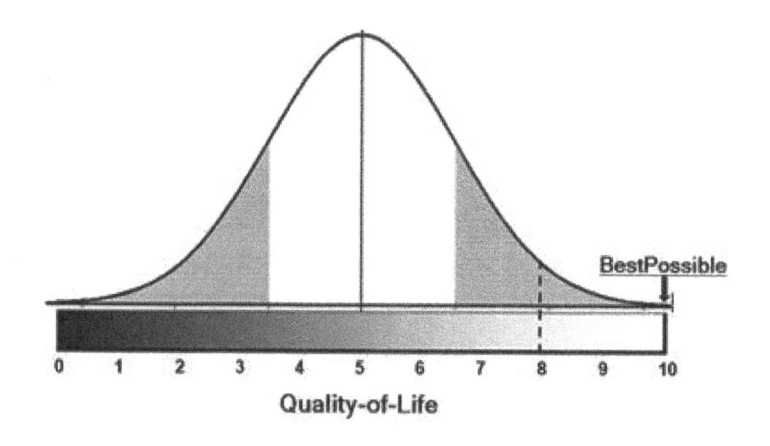

Part Three-Your BestPossible Self

Your Masterpiece

We are all artists and our own masterpieces. Through our thoughts, choices, and actions, we continually reshape who we are and will be. But our freewill lets us do makeovers any time along our life journeys.

What we think, choose, and do depend a lot on our philosophies and psychologies (chapter 8). With solid foundations in reality and the meaning of truth, we will each have a moral compass that will guide our artwork as we create wholesome lives and relationships.

BestPossible in a Troubled World

BestPossible is possible no matter our circumstances. However, how good life can be varies a lot among political environments along with all other factors. Citizens of nations ranked high on lists according to personal and economic freedom have many advantages, but so do less free people of high desire, motivation, and creativity.

The BestPossible concepts and opportunities apply to all people whether they enjoy free-world liberties or are confined by tyrants or prison walls. We all live in two worlds—our private inner world and our physical outer worlds—and the BestPossible concepts apply to both. Our true selves, our souls, reside internally. Whatever is happening in troubled parts of the world, we each remain free to make our inner spiritual world and our outer spheres of influence as peaceful as they can be.

Master of Destinies

The outcomes of our many endeavors and journeys through time are not predestined; they are all the results of our freewill choices and actions. We can make them whatever we choose. Our lives are not events with predestined outcomes. Rather, they are lifelong series of endeavors and relationships subject to our freewill and choices. Their outcomes are largely up to each of us. When you deliberately choose to define and make BestPossible your goal, you take control of your destiny.

Destination BestPossible

As long as there is life on Earth, there will be change. Many fear and resist change by clinging to traditions and what's known. While traditions promote stability, they often have adverse effects as the world changes around us. Most often, it is best to welcome changes and know that with them come fresh, new opportunities.

Change is why journeys to BestPossibles are endless for those who choose to keep moving forward. People who feel good about themselves, their missions, and life in general want challenges. They want to be the best they can be. As long as we are serving noble missions, there can be no journey more rewarding than one aimed deliberately at destination BestPossible.

Continuous Liberation

Liberation comes mainly from our creativity. Traditional practices confine us to traditional results. New thinking and

Part Three—Your BestPossible Self

ideas liberate us to achieve more rewarding and exciting results. The way to make steady progress is to deliberately and systematically make our BestPossibles better. A key feature of BestPossible is that it is time dependent: it changes with time. It depends on current circumstances, which are subject to nature and self-initiated change. Consequently, as we work to define and go for the best we can be, we should enjoy knowing that even as we act, we are stretching our horizons. When setting off for destination BestPossible, you will be creating personal excitement, enthusiasm, and confidence that work to enable accelerated success and a continual process of making your BestPossible better.

On the Bright Side of Life

Mother Nature means for our lives to be wonderful and exciting and it is up to each of us to make them so. To keep wonder and excitement alive, we must move toward brightness in all that we do.

BestPossible Is Forever

BestPossible is forever in two ways. First, it is not something to do until something better comes along. By its very definition nothing can be better than BestPossible. Fads come and go, but basic truths stand unaltered by time; there always will be a BestPossible level of achievement for every undertaking.

Second, our own BestPossibles are forever because as we approach them, we gain experience, skills, wisdom, and perspectives that allow new and better BestPossibles to appear on the horizon.

Nature's Call to Action

Only we humans survive and live by freewill. We are on our own as nature calls on us to discover BestPossible living.

In Harmony with Nature

As my last conclusion, I can say with humble gratitude that all the ideas that I've covered in this book are lessons and facts from nature. In chapter 8, I talk about nature-based philosophy in which reality is acknowledged as real, knowledge is truth, and ethics and morality respect and wholesomely promote human life. Nature enables BestPossible survival and advancement for all life forms. Given this easily verifiable fact, what I call BestPossible living is fully in tune with nature.

Epilogue

Dreams of the Future

It is part of our nature to dream of ways to make our lives better. We all need something to look forward to; that's what keeps us going.

From the beginning of our time on planet Earth, needs and longings to make things better have been behind all human ingenuity, inventions, and progress. We have come a long way from being cave dwellers to being explorers of outer space, and most of our advancements have been in the last 250 years.

There are now more than 120 democracies in the world. This number is close to two-thirds of our world's nations. Where there is freedom to vote, there is enough personal liberty for people to have dreams and to act purposefully to turn those dreams into realities. Along with this expanding freedom have come scientific and technical achievements that have contributed greatly to our comfort and health. More importantly, under the ideals of freedom and equal opportunity,

Discover BestPossible Living

more of us than ever before can visualize and work to create lives of greater happiness and quality of life.

Free of self-imposed limitations and restraints, our dreams become dreams of BestPossible living. Although BestPossible living will always be different among people, it remains accessible to those of all nations who choose to dream and reach as high as their perceptions and aspirations allow. Given a choice, most people would rather dream and go for what they perceive as achievable BestPossible lives than impossible fantasies.

From its start The United States of America has been an anomaly among nations. Shortly after the age of reason and the Enlightenment, our Founding Fathers created a nation that honored the natural rights of its individual citizens and constituted a government of the people, by the people, and for the people. This new freedom-based nation was soon populated by self-vetted immigrants—ambitious, creative, freedom-loving souls risking all in pursuit of the American dream. America is no longer an anomaly. With the continuing spread of democracy, increasing numbers of people are being liberated to follow their own kinds of dreams.

Because natural law is on the side of all that is good, Mother Nature will inevitably have her way. As the people of our world increasingly discover and learn to enjoy the unlimited fruits of BestPossible living, their nations will become more peaceful and prosperous. This in turn will make everyone's BestPossibles increasingly better.

Epilogue-Dreams of the Future

Because going for *better* is part of human nature, it is timeless and bodes well for the future of life on planet Earth. Although there have been and be setbacks, life for our future generations will become increasingly bright along their journeys through time.

Endnote

There's a story beyond my greased-pole story (see preface). In the summer of 1942, I lived with my family in a wartime housing project on Brookdale Avenue about two blocks from San Francisco's newly opened **Cow Palace**. Shortly after the bombing of Pearl Harbor, the six-acre structure was put to use by the US Army for preparation and embarkation of soldiers going to the Pacific Theater.

The city was prepared for air attacks with all streetlights covered with cone-shaped hoods attached with two rubber straps. One morning after a windy night I came out to find the hood of the streetlight by our apartment hanging by one strap. By the end of the day I had a plan to shimmy the pole and snap the loose strap back into place. In my imagination I had protected at least a thousand soldiers and our whole neighborhood from an easily targeted night bombing raid. In my mind I was a quiet, unsung hero ready for more action.

For me that San Francisco summer is full of memories that have fed into the *magic of now* to this day. That greased pole climb and its indelible inner rewards have allowed me to savor my *present* even as I've stayed busy *inventing* best-possible futures.

This book is more than just another collection of thoughts and ideas. It is a collaboration with Mother Nature meant to help its readers to literally achieve their full potentials for inner peace and prosperity. This book is a down payment on my payback and pay-it-forward for all the joy and fulfillment that nature and the people in my life have made possible along my life's journey.

If you have enjoyed and gained value from Discover BestPossible Living I suggest you consider sharing it with your family and friends as a form of thanks for things they have done for you and an act of pay-it-forward for those who may pass on your good deed. Word-of-mouth has always been the surest way to promote good-reads. With the Internet-based Facebook and other social media, word-of-mouth has taken on a whole new meaning. Now, recommendations and book comments and reviews cover the world in seconds.

If you enjoyed and gained value from this book, please take a moment to leave a quick review on Amazon.com

Appendix A

Chapter Highlights

*Whatever the mind can conceive
and believe, it can achieve.*

—Napoleon Hill

This appendix is offered to serve as convenient refresher. I'm an avid highlighter whenever I read meaty nonfiction. Here you will find points I deem worthy of special attention and revisits from the three parts of this book.

Whether nature comes from a supreme creator, from evolution, or from a combination of causes, it is what it is; it's to be seen, studied, recognized, and honored—or not. This fact that nature exists independent of personal beliefs and perceptions means the insights and lessons of this book can be studied, accepted, and applied by readers of all persuasions, religious or not.

Part One – Wonders of Human Nature

Quite wonderfully, Mother Nature has been equipping humans with tools and incentives for BestPossible survival and advancement for more than fifty thousand years.

BestPossible is a universally applicable concept for all human endeavors. Our freewill lets us think, make decisions, and act during our time in this world as prosperously and enjoyably as possible. The more skilled we become at leading optimal lives, the more we are able to contribute to the well-being of our communities and nations and the entire world.

Unlike plants and animals that live optimally by biological programming and instincts, we humans are anomalies; we are naturally endowed with mental tool kits we use by freewill to determine the quality of our lives. Achieving a BestPossible life happens by choice.

Chapter 1 – The Power of Purpose

* Our lives are strings of purposeful actions. We determine the quality of our lives by our choices of purposes and their resulting actions and achievements.
* Recognized or not, every human action has purpose. From the rhythmic beats of our hearts to our pursuits of lifelong missions, we act involuntarily or deliberately with purpose.
* The most important issue is how wholesome our purposes are. To live good lives, we must be good people with wholesome values and motives.

Appendix A - Chapter Highlights

* According to nature's plan, her purpose for our time on earth is to practice BestPossible living. This serves nature's purpose of peaceful and prosperous propagation of humans, her most complex of all life forms.
* Given the above, nature-based life purposes can serve as generic foundations for all people who choose to live as wholesome contributors to their communities, their world, and their own wellbeing.
* By way of our freewill, we are responsible for choosing the purposes that determine our actions and the quality of our lives.
* When discussing and naming good and evil, there are no shades of gray. A person's purposes and actions either promote lives in tune with nature or they detract. Good people sometimes do bad things by mistake; evil people repeatedly do bad things on purpose. They use their freewill to work against nature.
* Both love and hate are internally felt emotions derived from value judgments. This is their only similarity. Love is the ultimate in benevolence; hate is the ultimate in malevolence. Love is the most life-promoting of all emotions. It is experienced as a positive, healthy emotion that is right and good in every way. Hate is love's direct opposite. It is the darkest of all emotions. Contrary to promoting life, hate detracts from life with inevitable negative consequences for its perpetrators.
* Movement in status is a journey through time. People perform best when they can visualize where they have been, where they are, and where they are going.

Discover BestPossible Living

* All our endeavors can be viewed as journeys represented by continuum with dark ends and BestPossible bright ends separated by shades of gray.
* The power of purpose is felt up close and personal as we shape who we are and how we choose to live.

Chapter 2 – The Nature of BestPossible

* BestPossible is not something to do until something better comes along. For us under current circumstances nothing can be better. But our BestPossibles get better as we get better.
* For our successes to have meaning, we must have destinations; actions without purpose are wastes of time.
* Between our present position and BestPossible are all our opportunities for improvement; there is no place else to look.
* Whatever continuum that applies at the moment, please recognize that between where you judge yourself to be positioned and your self-defined BestPossible is your ready-for-harvest field of opportunity.
* BestPossible is forever in two ways: First, BP is not something to do until something better comes along. By its definition, nothing can be better. Fads come and go, but basic truths stand unaltered by time; there is and always will be a BestPossible level of achievement for every undertaking. Second, BP is forever because as we advance

Appendix A-Chapter Highlights

we gain experience, skills, and wisdom that cause new and better BestPossibles to appear on the horizon.

Chapter 3 – Our Gift of Freewill

* We humans are nature's only creatures who survive and advance by freewill. This means we have to choose to live BestPossible lives. It also means there is no limit to how great we can make our lives.
* As another aspect of our being anomalies of nature, only we can act toward our own destruction while enjoying the process right up to our demise. We are happy when pursuing our values, however destructive they may be. Rationalization, secondhand living, and indoctrinations (brainwashing) are among common natural traps.
* Perhaps the most positive part of our being anomalies is that we are, by design or default, masters of our own destinies.
* Mother Nature grants us only one entitlement: freewill.
* Although we humans are innately equipped with all the tools we need to live at the BestPossible ends of our many continuums, we come into the world without instructions. Each of us must learn how to use our tool kits, even as we face a world of endless possibilities and hazards. How well we do this determines our levels of success and happiness along our life journeys.
* We can achieve BestPossible in things we choose to do. But because we live by choice and freewill, we must first

learn how to know what is possible and then how to make it happen.

Chapter 4 – The Creation of Circumstances

* BestPossible recognizes all circumstances. The better we plan and control our circumstances, the better our BestPossibles.
* It's better to face planned circumstances than unplanned ones, but either can prove to be advantageous. Planning is all about predetermining circumstances.
* Course adjustments and changes are normal parts of optimal living. It's a process of gaining advantages from the unfolding of unplanned, unforeseeable circumstances.

Chapter 5 – Gifts of Cognition and Reason

* Our nature-endowed tool kits serve many functions. Two master tools coordinate all others: nature's gifts of cognition and reason. These gifts are to be nurtured and cherished all the years of our lives.
* Our brains are unbelievable in what they can do. While they remain busy taking care of our bodily functions, they stand ready to serve our developmental and social needs.
* We have these tools from birth, but it is up to each of us to learn and master their use. This is especially true for cognition and reason because we use them to integrate our other

Appendix A-Chapter Highlights

tools to gain knowledge and wisdom and to solve problems we encounter throughout our lives.

* Our education starts at birth and grows throughout our lifetimes. Whatever our goals, improved cognition, reasoning, and gained knowledge broaden our fields of opportunity.
* How well we learn to live and enjoy our years depends greatly on how well we learn to use our nature-endowed tool kits, especially our gifts of cognition and reason. These are and always will be our primary problem solvers; they connect our inner and outer worlds and enable us to perceive, decide, and act in our own best interests as we optimally serve the needs and interests of others.

Chapter 6 – Rewards of Success

* With every success come spiritual and material profits. We need profits of both forms to fuel our life journeys.
* Universal law is part of nature and is binding upon human actions. Based on observation and simple logic, three corollary natural laws of profit can be identified and named.
* The three laws of profit apply to both our material and spiritual worlds. While material gains are important and often essential for advancement, it's only our spiritual rewards that shape what really counts when all is said and done. Other than making us happy and adding the self-esteem that comes with personal achievement, fancy cars and big houses are nothing more than stuff. It's how they make us feel about ourselves that matters.

* Prosperity is a state of flourishing that comes with ongoing successes and their flow of profits and acquired resources. All come as peaceful spiritual rewards and worldly external rewards. Here, peace feeds prosperity and prosperity feeds peace: they always work together and are always tied closely to our profit imperative.

Part Two – Nature of Self-Creation

Through her gift of freewill, Mother Nature enables each of us to create the person we choose to be.

Chapter 7 – Your Artistic Self

* We are all artists, and our most important works are the creations of our own persons. Each of us will be a work in progress throughout the years of our lives.
* Everything we think, do, and say throughout our lives in some measure affects what kind of person we are at any point in time.
* Your "artwork" and resulting character will first and foremost reflect your basic values. These in turn will manifest in your deeds, integrity, and wholesomeness and in the health of your worldview.
* We add depth and interest to our characters with our diversities of experience. Through the adventures of our friendships, education, reading, travel, and vacations, we create in ourselves new dimensions to our beings.

Appendix A-Chapter Highlights

* Your character shows physically in your demeanor, laughter, posture, manner of speaking, and many other subtle ways. But what make up the essence of who you are your core values; they show in your sense of life and how you view the world and the people you know.
* Your self-image and self-esteem play integral roles in your life. Most importantly, by building self-esteem you enhance your views of your future.
* We build our self-esteem by staying true to our moral compasses and choosing and achieving worthy purposes.
* As artists all, we invariably show our values in our work. When others respond favorably to our creations, it is because they share some of our core values.
* Your "artwork" includes creating the days and years of your life. Being at the helm of your life, you are the one who must steer your way into the future.
* Depending on your starting place, your "artwork" may be a makeover more than a from-scratch composition. Either way your rewards for success can be just as satisfying.
* BestPossible living comes as result of creating and being a BestPossible person.

Chapter 8 – Your Philosophical and Psychological Selves

* Each of us has a philosophy. Without one we would be adrift with no rudder or anchor.

* We each have a psychology to help us find our way and stay on course.
* No matter where we start out, we can reshape our philosophies, psychologies, and resulting value judgments at any time; there's always a way, and it's never too late to realign.
* If Mother Nature was an actual woman, she would live by a philosophy that is totally aligned with that of Mother Nature, the nonperson.
* Reality is what it is, independent of how it might be perceived by an individual or the majority of a society.
* Our psychologies are our mental characteristics and attitudes. All human behavior is psychological and subjective. One's actions are subject to one's personal perceptions of reality, purpose, priorities, circumstances, and myriad other factors.
* Your philosophy is your social and moral guidance system.

Chapter 9 – Your Spiritual and Physical Selves

* We all simultaneously reside within two worlds. We live in our own inner spiritual world and our outer physical world.
* The essence of you is your spiritual self; it directs your choices and actions. Your spiritual self chooses how you interact with your outside world.

Appendix A-Chapter Highlights

* Your inner self connects with your physical self in order to pursue your purposes within the material world.
* Recognized or not, everything we do throughout our days is the result of someone's creativity. BestPossible living requires you to be the primary creator in your use of time.

Chapter 10 – Your Rational and Emotional Selves

* Reason is your basic tool for advancement. It keeps you grounded in reality. Your emotions tell you how you're doing and reward your successes.
* Reason plays many roles in keeping us out of trouble and on safe ground. We use our reasoning power to discern what is true and what is not and to stay grounded in reality. Reason helps us make small and large decisions as we navigate through life.
* Emotions play equally important roles. They are mental, spiritual, and physical effects of value-directed thoughts and actions. Emotions keep us alive and make us want to stay that way. They reward good behavior and punish bad choices.
* Emotional feedback plays an essential role when we initiate actions. It tells us how well we are honoring prior value judgments.

* This is a good rule of thumb to remember: reason-based emotions are healthy; emotional-based actions make us vulnerable.

Chapter 11 – Your Social Self

* BestPossible is by definition worthy, wholesome, and moral.
* Because we are a gregarious species, we are naturally sociable; we seek and enjoy the company of others. Because of this nature, interacting with fellow humans is an essential part of BestPossible living. In fact this is one of our greatest sources of pleasure and meaningful achievements.
* The basics of nature-based morality are the surest, safest, and best components for our personal moral foundations. There can be no others that effectively address the issues of right versus wrong, good versus evil, and love versus hate.
* What are noble objectives when making decisions? The answer is found within the laws of nature and the nature of wholesome goals and action. Anything that promotes life is wholesome; anything that detracts from or destroys life acts against nature: in the absence of life, there is no issue of morality.
* Ignorance is at the root of evil for both perpetrators and their victims.
* Love and hate are polar-opposite emotions. Love is pro-nature; hate is anti-nature. Love is healthy; hate harms

Appendix A - Chapter Highlights

  health. Love breeds love; hate breeds hate. Love celebrates life; hate works against life.
* Natural morality tends to come with common sense. This is because of lessons we learned as infants and adolescents about survival and success. When we are close to nature, we learn a lot about reality. Natural morality is tied directly to reality and the laws of nature.
* Good people find great happiness in making other good people happy. The pursuit of happiness is a key part of human nature, and perhaps the greatest source of happiness is found in making others happy.

Chapter 12 – Your Enterprising Self

* Your life is an enterprise of many purposes. You play all roles from CEO to janitor.
* An entrepreneur plans and manages an enterprise. An enterprise is a complex undertaking involving considerable risk. By these definitions, everyone's life is an enterprise, and we're all entrepreneurs with the complex task of ever-challenging life management.
* If we had no constraints in life, we would have no rewarding challenges, no fields of opportunity. Instead of being happy, we would be bored silly.
* Perhaps the most essential key to wellbeing and happiness is healthy self-esteem. When you prove to yourself you are able to take care of yourself while accomplishing

significant things, your self-esteem gets a big boost. This puts great importance on achieving success as CEO of your own enterprise.
* Successful life management not only leads to fiscal independence, but also builds feelings of self-worth that are essential for inner health and happiness. This makes being a well-performing, enterprising self an important part of BestPossible living.

Part Three – Your BestPossible Self

We are naturally equipped to lead BestPossible lives. To discover and enjoy your BestPossible self is to go with the flow of nature.

Every life endeavor takes place along a journey through time, however short or long. BestPossible living means deliberately clearing the way so all our journeys are full of adventure and joy. Optimal living may seem like a daunting endeavor; however, it is not as hard as most would think. First, it is important to remember that there is a way to live BestPossibly whatever our age and situation. As an anomaly of nature, you can in fact determine the destinies of your life journeys.

Chapter 13 – The Magic of Now

* Our pasts, presents, and futures have much to offer. There's magic in the fact that we can visit and gain from all three in our now.

Appendix A–Chapter Highlights

* We can look at time in three dimensions: past, present, and future. A marvelous thing about our minds is that we can visit and live in any one of the three dimensions whenever we want.
* Without what I call the magic of now, our lives would go nowhere. We call on what we've learned in our past to live in our present and to plan our todays and tomorrows.
* When you choose to consciously and vividly go back in time, you experience past events from more mature perspectives. Because you now have more knowledge and wisdom, you are able to draw fresh lessons by mentally reliving achievements and correcting mistakes.
* How we see ourselves helps shape our futures. What we achieve first appears as images of success. This means we can invent our own futures by visualizing in vivid detail what we want those futures to be.
* When tapping into the magic of now to prelive specific aspects of your future, the more vivid and enjoyable you make your experiences, the more certainly and enjoyably they will become your reality.
* *Now* is a fleeting, infinitely small slice of time, yet it is all we have to get things done. All our past and current achievements have been done during strings—or periods—of time, just as all our future accomplishments will be. This means living in the now is more of a metaphor than a reality. But it's a good, highly useful metaphor. Living in the now is about consciously enjoying and savoring present moments, however long they happen to be.

Discover BestPossible Living

* You have a paradigm that defines the limits of your self-selected playing field and your assumed rules for success. Because your paradigm is a map that resides in your conscious and subconscious minds, it is fully malleable. By exercising your freewill, you can change and reshape it any time.
* Whatever your paradigm, within its limits are untapped opportunities and rewards waiting to be captured and enjoyed. BestPossible living includes creatively stretching boundaries and challenging rules to liberate ourselves from overly restrictive perceptions and assumptions of current paradigms.
* Time exists only in the now. Now is the only time we have to use, but it's a magical time. Besides re-enjoying the best of our pasts, we can prelive our futures even as we live and savor our here and now.

Chapter 14 – Purposes, Goals, and Waypoints

* BestPossible is a universal beacon that lights your way toward your purpose.
* Because all our actions have purpose, we all, in fact, live purpose-driven lives. It is our choices of what to do with our time and our levels of success that determine how well we live.
* The value we deliver to our world through our jobs or careers, relationships, and civic involvements can more

than fulfill any needs we may feel to contribute and earn our ways through life. It can be very satisfying, even if we never find more noble purposes.

* There is enough meaning in life without having to be rich and famous, making earthshaking contributions, or leaving long-remembered legacies.
* That said, it is through our long-term and lifetime missions that we can gain the greatest fulfillment and deliver the most value to our world.
* Only you know what is right and possible for you. Only you know your ambitions, aspirations, desires, and basic values.
* It doesn't matter if you understate or overstate your potential because doing better happens on your way to BestPossible. What's important is that you perceive an outcome to be achievable and desirable. Whatever you accept as your targeted BestPossible is sure to get better along your way as you gain experience, skills, and broader and closer perspectives.
* While visualizing what is achievable and believable, our minds are also seeing how to do it. In this way we visualize BestPossible road maps for getting from where we are to where we can and would like to be. In doing so we create previews of paths of least resistance.
* Long-term goals are journeys best traveled by way of predefined interim waypoints and milestones.
* This creation and visualization process is universally applicable to all human advancement. We need to see

ourselves in our desired futures. Without such images we have no motivation to change the status quo.

Chapter 15 – Your Life Journeys

* Each person's life journey is composed of countless sub-journeys, each with its own challenges, rewards, and disappointments.
* Every person's life journey comes in parts. According to our choices, we travel many parallel and diverse journeys.
* Nature endows us with freewill and allows us to choose where and how we will travel.
* Our physical and spiritual selves are distinct but inseparable. They go everywhere together; they travel through time as a joint entity.
* Whether physical or spiritual, the journey metaphor works for any movement beyond where we are toward where we would choose to be.
* You venture into the physical world to carry out your plans and to interact with others.
* Because time is limited and precious, it is important that you choose your journeys and supportive actions carefully, based on your own freewill and personally embraced values.
* Your quality of life reflects the sum of your worldly and spiritual achievements. The ultimate measure is spiritual. Its rewards are the warmth of inner glow, lasting peace of mind, and pervasive happiness.

Appendix A-Chapter Highlights

* There are no hard-and-fast constraints on your various BestPossibles. All hurdles and roadblocks will yield to your creativity; you can always get there from here.

Chapter 16 – Three Golden Keys

* Keys are for gaining access to something special. What can be more special than a BestPossible life?
* Key Number One—Be Your BestPossible Self
    * Self-creation is a matter of fact: by your lifetime of choices and actions, you are who you made yourself to be.
    * It is important to note and remember that your masterpiece is a work in progress that can be changed and made over anywhere along your way.
    * Being firmly in touch with reality is necessary for a nature-based philosophical foundation.
    * Core values of honesty, fairness, trust, justice, and integrity come before optimal living. Without these basics, pursuits of personal values will inevitably lead to more harm than good.
    * As CEO of your personal enterprise, life management offers your greatest challenges and rewards.
    * BestPossible use of the first key calls for you to plan and use your days and years for purposes that will yield high levels of inner peace and prosperity along your various life journeys.
* Key Number Two—Live BestPossible Days and Years

* To be a BestPossible person is to lead a BestPossible life. Plan ahead and wake up each morning with the deliberate intent to make this a BestPossible day.
* Everything you do has purpose, consciously recognized or not. The more careful and deliberate you are at choosing purposes and their supportive actions, the more able you will be to direct your efforts toward what is truly BestPossible.
* To go for BestPossible, you first need to know what it looks like. Only you can know this.
* While living BestPossible days and years, most of your time will be spent tending to the business of your personal enterprise.
* It's always tempting to service what appears to be the most urgent at the expense of the most important.
* Record keeping serves many essential functions. This is especially true when planning and managing for BestPossible near- and long-term futures.
* Key Number Three—Celebrate Your Successes
  * When moving toward honorable goals, every step forward is a success worthy of celebration.
  * Steps forward and daily achievements are all successes that get rewarded with pleasing moments of reflection and restful sleep.
  * Celebrations of success provide lasting incentives for continuing success. They also help confirm that our efforts are on track.

* These golden keys are mental concepts for gaining access to a world of spiritual freedom and liberty. They have the power to unlock self-imposed shackles and free us to achieve our true potential in all that we choose to do.

Chapter 17 – Taking Flight

* To launch the process of BestPossible living is not hard—all it takes is clearly informed intent, determination, and proclamation.
* To handle and overcome inevitable discouraging setbacks, it is good to remember that success is a journey and is not about arrival at a destination.
* Skilled piloting of airplanes is in many ways analogous to BestPossible living. It involves most of the ingredients and dimensions required for purposeful, skillful and safe life management.
* Flying always involves well-defined purposes, careful planning, awareness of and heeds to risks and dangers, tending to unfolding circumstances, observance of rules, recognition and honoring laws of nature, codes of ethics, navigation skills, and constant demands for free-will choices.
* There are four kinds of forces that affect all things that fly. They are: weight; lift; thrust; and drag. Just as these four forces are always there for all birds, butterflies, and

Discover BestPossible Living

pilots, it is helpful to be aware that these same forces come into play throughout our personal lives.

* Planning and traveling our life journeys is far more demanding and risky than flying airplanes, and yet we are expected to find our way and stay safe without an owner's manual.
* Diplomas are like pilot licenses in that they certify that their recipients are qualified to "fly up" to new levels learning and living.
* With sharply focused attention, study, and action, those working to become their best-possible selves will continue to gain qualifications, promotions, and added responsibilities. These advancements will not come with school-day diplomas but will be certified by self-awarded virtual licenses that speak loud-and-clear about who you are and what you have to offer.
* Preflight checklists are important but there is much more required. Because your "plane" is homebuilt you need to make sure it is well constructed, properly maintained, and equipped with the kind of moral compass that will guide you safely through periods of darkness and bad weather.
* BestPossible living is a process you must do one step, one day, one year at a time. As pilots fly one mile, one waypoint, and one destination at a time, they gain skills, learn lessons, make adjustments, build memories, and enjoy their successes all along their routes.
* Good Pilots never stop honing their skills. BestPossible living is like that — the better you get, the better your

Appendix A-Chapter Highlights

BestPossible gets. And your rewards for achievements never stop coming.
* Every success en route to BestPossible is a smooth landing worthy of celebration. Celebrations of successes are nature-based rewards that give incentives for more success, for survival, and for the assurance of human advancement.
* Beyond our today's physical air and space travel, our inner spiritual selves are without limits in what we can imagine and achieve.
* With our gifts of freewill, cognition, thought, and reason we can get the four forces of flight working in our favor to discover and truly enjoy the unending rewards of BestPossible living. And because our most meaningful and lasting rewards come to our inner selves, they lift our spirits to soar with eagles.

Chapter 18 — Nature-Based Conclusions

* We were born mentally equipped to lead best-possible lives. Because we have one life to live, it's important to make it the best it can be.
* We are all artists and our own masterpieces. Through our thoughts, choices, and actions, we continually reshape who we are and who we will be. But our freewill enables makeovers any place along our life journeys.
* By definition, we can be our BestPossible self but because we all live by freewill we must do it by choice.

Discover BestPossible Living

* BestPossible is possible no matter our circumstances. Whatever is happening in troubled parts of the world, we remain free to make our inner spiritual world as peaceful as it can be.
* The outcomes of our many undertakings and journeys through time are not predestined; they are results of our choices and resulting actions. When we deliberately choose to make BestPossible our goal, we take control of our destinies by making them what we want them to be.
* As long as we are serving noble missions, there can be no journey more rewarding than one aimed deliberately at Destination BestPossible.
* Liberation comes mainly from our creativity. New thinking and ideas liberate us for increasingly enjoyable lives. The way to make steady progress is to creatively and deliberately make our BestPossibles better.
* Mother Nature means for our lives to be wonderful and exciting and it's up to each of us to make it so. To keep wonder and excitement alive, we need to move toward brightness in all that we do.
* BestPossible is forever; there always will be a best-possible level of achievement for every undertaking. Our own BestPossibles are forever because as we approach them, we gain experience, skills, wisdom and perspectives that allow new and better BestPossibles to appear on the horizon.

Appendix A-Chapter Highlights

* I can say with humble gratitude that all I've covered in this book are lessons and facts from nature. Given that all of these are easily observed lessons and verifiable facts, what I call BestPossible living is a free-will process of discovering and following the lead of Mother Nature.

Appendix – B

Relevant Resources

Books

Allen, James. As a Man Thinketh. 1903

Blanchard, Ken and Spencer Johnson. The One Minute Manager. 1982

Byrne, Rhonda. The Secret. 2006

Canfield, Jack. The Success Principles. 2006

Chopra, Deepak. The Seven Spiritual Laws of Success. 1994

Covey, Stephen. Principle-Centered Leadership. 1990

Covey, Stephen. Seven Habits of Highly Effective People. 1989

Csikszentmihalyi, Mihaly. Flow: The Psychology of Optimal Experience. 1990

Gladwell, Malcolm. Outliers: The Story of Success. 2011

Johnson, Spenser. Who Moved My Cheese. 1998

Johnson, Spenser. The Precious Present. 1984

Kondo, Marie. The Life-Changing Magic of Tidying Up. 2014

Malts, Maxwell. Psycho-Cybernetics. 1960

Millman, Dan. No Ordinary Moments. 1992

Millman, Dan. The Laws of Spirit: A Tale of Transformation. 2010

Millman, Dan. Way of the Peaceful Warrior: A Book That Changes Lives. 2006

Peale, Norman Vincent. The Power of Positive Thinking. 1952

Rand, Ayn and Leonard Peikoff. Philosophy: Who Needs It. 1982

Tolle, Eckhart. The Power of Now: A Guide to Spiritual Enlightenment. 2004

Warren, Rick. The Purpose Driven Life. 2002

Weil, Andrew. Spontaneous Happiness, 2011

Documentary Films

First Footprints: The Original Pioneers of All Humankind. 2013

What the Bleep do We Know?! 2005

Internet Websites

www.bestpossible.com
www.bestpossible.com/blog/
www.facebook.com/BestPossibleBooks/

If you enjoyed and gained value from this book, please take a moment to leave a quick review on Amazon.com

About the Author

Dr. Eugene L. Bryan is best known for his groundbreaking work in the field of computer-based enterprise optimization—a technology he pioneered and refined over fifty-plus years as he helped hundreds of companies go for what he calls BestPossible performance. Gene now works through his company, BestPossible Solutions, as a consultant and author while continuing to advance, promote, and apply his advanced management concepts and supportive technologies.

Gene earned a bachelor of science degree from the University of Idaho, two master of science degrees from the University of California, Berkeley, and a PhD from the University of Michigan.

Before BestPossible Solutions, he founded and served as president and CEO of Decision Dynamics, Inc., where for thirty-two years, his company worked all over the United States and internationally, serving firms ranging from family-owned operations to Fortune 500 corporations.

Discover BestPossible Living

As a recognized enterprise-optimization expert, Dr. Bryan has delivered keynote speeches, seminars, and workshops in Canada, Chile, Mexico, France, the United Kingdom, New Zealand, and Australia, and throughout the United States. He has authored four books relating to the field of enterprise optimization.